Concepts and Strategies
for New Players

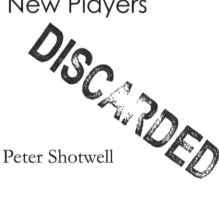

Peter Shotwell

TUTTLE PUBLISHING
Tokyo • Rutland, Vermont • Singapore

First published in 2006 by Tuttle Publishing, an imprint of Periplus Editions (HK) Ltd., with editorial offices at 364 Innovation Drive, North Clarendon, Vermont 05759.

Library of Congress Cataloging-in-Publication data
Shotwell, Peter, 1941–
    Go basics: concepts and strategies for new players / Peter Shotwell
        p. cm.
    Includes bibliographical references and index.
    ISBN-13: 978-0-8048-3688-3 (pbk.)
    ISBN-10: 0-8048-3688-4 (pbk.)
    1. Go (Game) I. Title
GV1459.5.S56 2005
794.4—dc22
           2005011419

Distributed by

North America, Latin America & Europe
Tuttle Publishing
364 Innovation Drive, North Clarendon, VT 05759-9436
Tel: (802) 773-8930; Fax: (802) 773-6993
info@tuttlepublishing.com
www.tuttlepublishing.com

Japan
Tuttle Publishing
Yaekari Building, 3rd Floor, 5-4-12 Osaki
Shinagawa-ku,Tokyo 141 0032
Tel: (03) 5437-0171; Fax: (03) 5437-0755
tuttle-sales@gol.com

Asia Pacific
Berkeley Books Pte. Ltd.
130 Joo Seng Road, #06-01, Singapore 368357
Tel: (65) 6280-1330; Fax: (65) 6280-6290
inquiries@periplus.com.sg
www.periplus.com

First edition
10 09 08 07 06
6 5 4 3 2 1

Printed in Singapore

TUTTLE PUBLISHING® is a registered trademark of Tuttle Publishing, a division of Periplus Editions (HK) Ltd.

Contents

Acknowledgments   8

Introduction   9
About Go 9
A Short History of Go 9
Playing Go 14
Some Important Information about This Book and 9 x 9 Go 17

PART ONE
The Opening Game and the Mechanics of Go   **19**

CHAPTER 1: Starting to Play   **21**
The Opening Moves 21
Capture: The One Basic Rule of Go 22

CHAPTER 2: The Art of Capture   **25**
Capturing on the Edge of the Board 25
Capturing in the Corners 27
Capturing in the Middle of the Board 28
A Review of Capturing 29
The Capturing Game 31

CHAPTER 3: All about Ladders   **33**
Double Atari 34
The Ladder 36
Some Ladder Exercises 37

CHAPTER 4: Ladder Breakers, Loose Ladders, and Nets 39
Ladder Breakers 39
Nets and Loose Ladders 42

CHAPTER 5: Clever Moves   **45**
Some Tesuji Exercises 48

PART TWO
The Middle Game and the Strategies of Go   51

CHAPTER 6: Life with Two Eyes and Thinking Territorially 53
Understanding Eyes 57
False Eyes 59

CHAPTER 7: Dead or Alive?   62
Live and Dead Shapes 62
Some Examples of Life and Death 65
Live Groups in the Corners, Sides, and Center 68

CHAPTER 8: Running Fights in Sente and Gote   70
Reverse and Double Sente 74

CHAPTER 9: Ko and Seki   76
Ko 76
Ko Threats 77
Seki 80

PART THREE
The Endgame   83

CHAPTER 10: The Endgame I: The Beginner's Way   85
Aji 86
Two Simple but Wrong Ways to Play the Endgame 88

CHAPTER 11: The Endgame II: The Professional Way   92
A Professional Endgame 93
Continuing to the End 98
A Review of the Game 100

PART FOUR
Advancing in Go   103

CHAPTER 12: Harnessing the Powers of Sacrifice   105
Sacrificial Maneuvering 105
A Bigger Sacrifice 108

CHAPTER 13: **A Big Ko**   **112**
Cross-Cuts 114
Hunting Down a Big Group 122
A Mistake in Ko 124
An Exercise 125

CHAPTER 14: **Invading: Why, When, and Where?**   **126**
Opening in the Center 126
Invasions 129

CHAPTER 15: **On to the Big Board: A Review of Go**
    Basics   **134**

APPENDIX

Getting Started with Igowin   **139**
All about Ranks 141
Games with Igowin 143
25-Kyu 144
18-Kyu 145
17-Kyu 147
16-Kyu 148
15-Kyu 150
13-Kyu 151
Getting Better at Go 153

GLOSSARY   **155**

RECOMMENDED READING   **158**

ABOUT THE AMERICAN GO ASSOCIATION   **159**

Acknowledgments

First and foremost, I want to thank my editor, Jennifer Brown, who with others at Tuttle suggested writing this book and who was instrumental in helping to shape and edit it.

Guo Juan, a 6-dan professional from China and many times European Open champion, who now teaches via the Internet in Amsterdam, was generous in providing professional analyses of the even games. However, any mistakes must be attributed to my misinterpretation or oversights, since she could not go over the manuscript. Her teaching skills are unrivaled, and she can be reached for personal instruction at www.goschool.tk.

Sy Cassorla and Bjorn Olson read through an initial manuscript and provided very useful comments.

Old friends Roy Laird, Chris Garlock, Terry Benson, Ron Snyder, Barbara Calhoun, Jean Claude Chetrit and others from the Brooklyn Go Club (www.brooklyngoclub.org) and the American Go Association offered cogent advice.

As always, Richard Bozulich from Kiseido Publications was extremely helpful.

Many thanks to Anders Kierluff, whose Smart Go program (www.smartgo.com) enabled the game files to be beautifully rendered into print.

Lastly, as with my first book, without support from my wife, Susan Long, and her parents, George and Pearl Schweitzer, producing this book would have been very much harder, and I am very grateful.

Introduction

About Go

Long known as the most complex and subtle, yet simplest and most beautiful of games, Go has captivated hundreds of millions of people throughout history. No one knows who "invented" it, but Go-like playing could go back four thousand years, as indicated by small piles of lozenge-shaped "game" stones buried next to bodies in ancient Chinese tombs. Since then, it has become intertwined with Eastern and Western philosophy, religion, literature, art, and science. Now, millions of games are played every year on Internet game sites, as well as in clubs and homes around the world.

With only one simple rule—which generates a complexity that baffles the best of computer programs—Go is more than a game. Having a handicap system that makes every game exciting, it has survived so long not just because it is fun and challenging, but because players also believe it enhances their mental, artistic, and even spiritual lives.

A Short History of Go

Go and its "rule"—or rather principle—of surrounding has always been a metaphor for many things in China. In early myths, it was said to have been brought "down from the Heavens" by the god-king Yao to educate his first-born son about 2200 BC. Perhaps symbolizing an evolution in human consciousness and strategic planning, he and his people might have seen Go first as a hunting game, and then, as times changed, as symbolic of agricultural

activity in the square fields, with the stones metaphorically blocking and releasing the flow of water.

A thousand years later, the Chinese religion changed to a sky
orientation. As attested to by poetic thought through the ages that
continues today, the "movement" of the black and white stones
reminded players of the sun and the moon, the constellations on
a map of the sky, and the passage of days and seasons.

Beginning about 500 BC, Taoist philosopher-warriors such as
Sun Tzu would have been managing the imbalances of yin and
yang and the flow of *qi* that were coursing over their playing
boards, as they thought these did in their wars, businesses, and the
rest of their lives. On the other hand, the Confucians and probably the early Buddhists looked at the playing of Go as a waste of
time and a corrupter of aristocratic youth because of the gam-
bling involved. By AD 500–1000, however, most of the rulers,
literati, warriors, and monks of China and Japan had elevated the
"Way of Go" to one of the "Four Arts"—along with painting,
music, and calligraphy. From that period on, those most successful in penetrating the "illusions of reality" on the "micro-world"
of the Go board were thought to be capable of doing the same in
the "real" world. By the early 1600s, this practical sentiment
impelled the first Japanese shoguns to sponsor four non-heredi-
tary "Go Houses" to study and play the game. For the next 350
years, their members scoured the countryside for young, talented
recruits to perpetuate themselves and beat their rivals. The top
player became the politically powerful teacher of the shoguns, and
the resulting competition took Go theory to unbelievable heights
of imagination and invention.

However, after the fall of the last shogun in the late nineteenth
century, it looked like the game, along with other artifacts of feu-
dalism, would be swept under the tidal wave of modernization.
Yet, ironically, it was this force that revived Go and brought the

game to undreamed popularity and prestige. As the early Taoists had found in their ancient world, the new leaders saw that the strategies for success they learned on their Go boards could be applied to the modern worlds of politics, war, and commerce. By the first part of the twentieth century, out-of-work and seemingly discarded professional players found themselves eagerly sought after to teach in schools, factories, and offices. Soon, newspapers with circulations in the millions were sponsoring well-paying, ruthless competitions. By dramatizing the exploits and rivalries of champion players, the game became one of the first mass-spectator sports in the world.

On the other side of the world, during the 1930s and 1940s, some chess players in the United States and Europe began to be aware that there was an equal or even superior game in their midst. After the Professional Japanese Go Association was reorganized on more "democratic" lines in the 1920s, it became instrumental in the worldwide spread of Go. It arranged tournaments in Europe and also helped the fledgling American Go Association with visits of top players and translations of key Go books and magazines. By the 1970s and 1980s, the number of Western Go enthusiasts began to grow in larger cities, and a diaspora of Chinese professionals came to live and teach in the West.

Meanwhile, the path toward a modern, popular, and sometimes frenzied attitude about Go took a different course in mainland China (where it was known as *Wei qi* or *Wei ch'i*). During the Cultural Revolution, Go was branded at best as a "bourgeois" activity. However, by the 1980s, millions of people were watching on their new TV sets as their formerly persecuted veteran and younger players began to beat, and finally dominate, the Japanese.

This wild popularity was repeated in Korea (where it is known as *Ba duk* or *Pa duk*). In the early 1990s, their players, some in their teens, also started beating not only the Japanese but also the Chinese. As had already happened in Japan, Go champions in Korea and China became rich, famous, and socially privileged. They were also emulated by thousands of children, some of whom would soon grow up to beat them. Large corporations took notice and began sponsoring many new international tournaments, some worth hundreds of thousands of dollars, and, for the last decade, these have mostly been won by Koreans.

However, with the coming of the Internet in the mid–1990s, Western players thought that Go faced another cultural crisis. Because of the prevalent feeling that the game was a spiritual and traditional exercise, best played with real boards and stones, they thought the game would be eclipsed in the new electronic age.

Instead, the Internet and the ease of play on computers caused an incredible spurt of popularity among young members of the computer generation. The Microsoft and Yahoo game sites, along with many dedicated servers, now enable people all over the world to play conveniently at any time. Over a thousand Web sites spread information about Go surveying the vast arena of professional and amateur games, tournaments, strategies, and history.

But, ironically in the computer age, Go has defeated the best efforts of programmers, and it remains a largely "for-humans-only" activity. Because the board is so "huge"—there may be more possible games than there are atoms in the universe—computers can be beaten by anyone after playing for only a few months. Human reasoning and pattern recognition are still needed to play good Go.

Meanwhile, the quality of Western amateur Go has considerably improved. The American and European Go associations receive generous funding from a Taiwanese millionaire and have been able to greatly expand their promotional activities. New books in English appear every month, and professional such as

Guo Juan (who helped on this book), maintain on-line teaching careers. With the encouragement of Japanese, Korean, and Chinese Go associations, dozens of Westerners have now turned professional.

Go has also entered the Western cultural mainstream. Memberships have surged in the American Go Association following appearances in books like *Shibumi, The Master of Go,* and *The Girl Who Played Go*; in TV programs such as *Wild Palms* and *Jag*; and in movies like *Pi, A Beautiful Mind,* and *The Go Masters.* In Japan, too, where Go was getting to be known as an "old persons' game," the hugely popular *Hikaru no Go* comic book and TV series (now available in English) has excited more interest in the game among youngsters than ever before.

Meanwhile, in the scientific and academic worlds, Go is being used in artificial intelligence studies and is contributing to the development of modern cognitive psychology. The independent arrangement of the groups of stones inspired the concept of surreal numbers, while analyses of the last few moves of the endgame have importantly figured in the development of combinatorial game theory. Most recently, physicists have been using linked-computer Go-playing programs to tackle protein folding problems in chaos theory, and Go-playing astronauts have brought the game into space.

In short, countless generations have thought Go was something "good to do" for many reasons. We hope you will, too. Welcome to the world of Go!

Playing Go

People often ask, "Is Go like chess?" No. Go is a radically different game that is more like a mental martial art—with the emphasis on *art*. Go deals with illusive *shapes* and *patterns* of groups that are built up with stones placed on the board, so Go players routinely say that good play involves the "balance" and "harmony" of its elements.

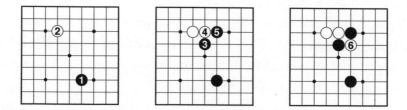

This is how the first instructional game in the book starts out on page 21. The board starts out empty and players begin to put lozenge-shaped stones down on the board, one by one. The pieces do not move after that.

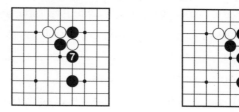

By the time the seventh move has been made, it is clear how the animating principle of Go works—surrounding a stone will *capture* it. As in the diagram on the right, if Black can make the move marked by the triangle, the white stone will be removed from the board and become a prisoner of Black. More will be said about this later.

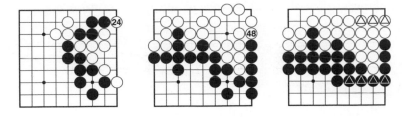

As the game progresses, it is also easy to see how intertwining groups that are interacting with each other form out of the patterns of stones. By the time this mid-game position has been reached, Go is really getting exciting! You will have discovered by then how stones and groups can *die* in many ways, but also how they can *live*, when they surround empty spaces in certain ways.

As the first game concludes with move 48, it will become obvious that capture is really only a secondary feature of this amazing game, and that organizing *territory* is really what the game is all about.

Afterward, the stones are rearranged for easy counting. In the Western (originally the Japanese) way of counting, the *prisoners*— the marked stones that have been surrounded and taken up from the board—are put back to take away territory points from the player who lost them, and the scores are compared.

White controls the territory at the top, while Black has surrounded the empty intersections at the bottom. Black has more territory than White and has won the game, even after deducting some points for having moved first.

This game, which was played by two professionals in a Japanese fast-game TV tournament, takes up the first half the book. As it progresses, the basic techniques come alive on the board.

In the second half of the book there are four chapters that focus on games featuring more advanced strategies. These are difficult to learn quickly on bigger boards, but easy on the 9 x 9. They include the powers of sacrificing, using *ko* as a strategy, thinking territorially, and *invading* to set up a second, living group, as well as many other important concepts.

Last, there is an appendix featuring handicap games against Igowin, the 9 x 9 computer program in the AGA CD-ROM included with this book. If you are playing stronger players and must begin with handicap stones, as in the examples below, this is the place to take a look.

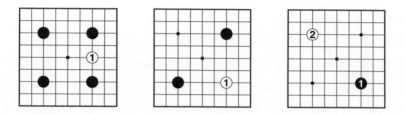

The appendix gives hints on how to reduce the initial handicap to zero and how to play against players stronger than Igowin. As with even play, it is much easier to learn the principles of handicap play on the 9 x 9 board than on bigger boards. And when you do graduate to them, your playing will be much less frustrating.

The book then concludes with information on where to find players and more books on Go, along with a list of activities of the American Go Association and how to contact them.

Some Important Information about This Book and 9 x 9 Go

Go is played on three different board sizes: the small 9 x 9 board, the 13 x 13 board, and the official 19 x 19 board. As one graduates to the different board sizes, the game's complexities and subtleties begin to unfold, providing a never-ending source of enjoyment as new levels of play are reached.

Beginning to play on the big 19 x 19 board is fun—any kind of Go is fun, after all. However, as I found out when I learned, if you start out on a full-sized board with no one to show you the principles of good play, it is easy to pick up bad habits that can take years to get rid of. This is why, in the West, it is considered easier to teach and learn to play Go on smaller, 9 x 9 boards.

This book takes that principle one step further and concentrates *only* on 9 x 9 Go. You'll find that the instruction in this book is almost entirely game-based because the games are simpler—something that is impossible to do with games on bigger boards. Rather than just listing principles, as beginner books usually do, the games in this book, all played by professionals, are specially chosen to demonstrate the basic tactics and strategies of Go. Go is a game, after all, and learning it, like learning a language, is best done with native speakers in the "land" where they live.

After taking your time and truly learning your way around the 9 x 9 board, you will have a solid basis for determining what the *big moves* and what the *small moves* are. This is because the basic principles of Go are true, no matter what the size of the board. The more advanced strategies you will be using on the bigger boards, such as choosing the right *joseki*, *fuseki* and *direction of play*, will not be undone by elementary mistakes that often spoil the games of beginners.

Another reason to stick to 9 x 9 Go for a period of time is that there is much more freedom to experiment while learning the fundamentals. Bad habits and wrong thinking, not identifiable on big boards because they are clouded over by territorial issues, become immediately evident on smaller ones. One of the oldest Go proverbs gives this advice: "Quickly lose your first hundred games." There is certainly no better or faster way to do that than on 9 x 9 boards! That said, let's start to play Go!

If you don't have a Go set, you can use colored beans, small candies, or washers on the board printed on page 160. Or better yet, enlarge it on a copy machine and play with pennies and dimes. (In fact, the white stones in Japanese sets are slightly smaller than the black ones, so they look the same size to the eye). You can also open up the recording program Gowrite in the AGA CD-ROM. Go to "File" and click "New." A choice of board sizes will appear. Then you can play electronically or click the "File Print" option to produce a board.

PART ONE

The Opening Game and the Mechanics of Go

Getting started in Go is easy, and in the process, you will find that your games will progress through three interesting stages: the *opening game*, the *middle game* and the *endgame*. Each has differing needs and characteristics.

Because even games start with an empty board, the opening is sometimes said to be the time when your "left brain" can artistically begin to "design" your game. As this happens and the groups start to emerge, it is a period when distant relationships between stones and an overall feeling for patterns seem to be more important than paying close attention to details.

CHAPTER ONE

Starting to Play

The Opening Moves

In a Go game, Black traditionally goes first and the players alternate moves afterwards, putting stones down on virtually any intersection they want.

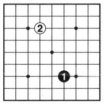 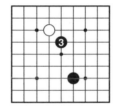 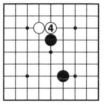

In this game, Black likes *influence* on the bottom and White likes it on the top. Black *approaches* with B3 and White *extends* with W4. In 19 x 19 Go, it is not considered good to approach right away, but it is commonly done on the 9 x 9 board. This is good for beginners, however, because it highlights the interactions of the stones, and teaches them the intricacies of maneuvering much faster. Something interesting is about to happen in the next few moves.

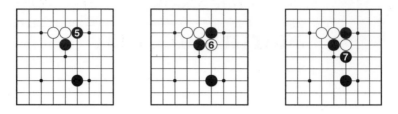

Black *blocks* White's progress with B5. White *cuts* with W6. After B7, the White stone is in danger of being *surrounded*.

Capture: The One Basic Rule of Go

The one basic rule in Go is: When a stone becomes surrounded, it is captured. By surrounding and capturing your opponent's stones, you will be able to gain more territory on the board, which is the ultimate object of the game. If a stone is surrounded, the Chinese say it has no *breaths* left. Westerners prefer to say that it has no *liberties*.

When a stone is captured, or *taken* as Go players say, it is picked up off of the board and becomes the prisoner of the other player. As will be shown later, when the score is counted at the end of the game, prisoners—the stones lost—will be subtracted from their original owner's territory.

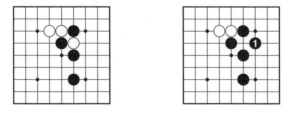

If Black played at B1, White's stone would be captured. It would be taken off the board as a prisoner. You can also say that the White stone would *die*.

In addition, if Black can keep control of the now empty inter-section for the rest of the game, Black will have also gained one point of territory on the board. Can the White stone avoid being surrounded by the Black stones?

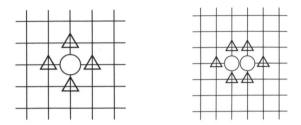

When White *attaches* to other White stones a *group* begins to form and becomes stronger because White has made it harder to be surrounded. Now the number of liberties—spaces around White—is six instead of four.

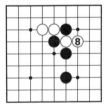

So White *runs away*. Surrounding by Black is now difficult.

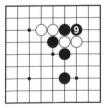

Black *chases*, still hoping to surround White.

Such is the beginning of a Go game. It is an opening that could have been played yesterday or four thousand years ago. Hopefully, it is also the beginning of a long relationship with the world's greatest board game!

CHAPTER TWO

The Art of Capture

Practice makes perfect! Now that you've been introduced to the basic play of the game, let's unravel some of the mysteries about capturing that will appear once you start to play.

Capturing on the Edge of the Board

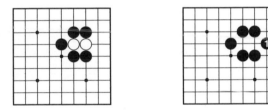

This is a hypothetical situation. With these and other "non-game" diagrams, just pretend that an instructor is laying stones out on the board for demonstration only. Here, close to the edge of the board, Black has managed to almost surround White. If it is Black's move, White will die. Black will have gained 2 prisoners and 2 points of territory for a total of 4. But Black does not have to capture immediately.

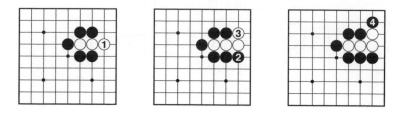

If it is White's move, White could try to run, but there isn't much room. After W1, White has three liberties, but it is Black's turn.

In the diagram on the right, White has only two liberties left.

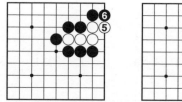
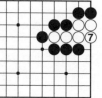
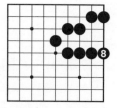

There is nowhere White can go. After B6, White has only one liberty and is therefore in *atari*. This is a Japanese word that means a stone can be taken on the next move. (Japanese terms and rules are used in Western Go because they introduced the game and promoted it.) Saying "atari" is similar to announcing "check" in chess. It is polite in beginners' games to warn of an impending capture, but it is usually not done in competitive situations.

W7 is a useless move because White would still be in atari and it would only add another stone to Black's prisoner pile. At any time, Black can capture.

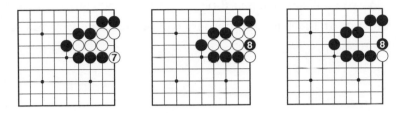

Suppose White tries this foolish move. Black can still take. Look at this situation carefully. It appears that in playing B8, Black would have no liberties, but it is Black's turn. Go is very logical, so Black can take before White can.

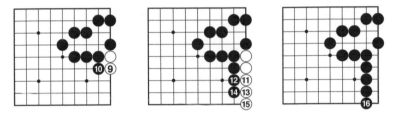

The lonely White stone that was left had only one liberty and was in atari. White could try to run, but it would do no good! B16 would extinguish the group.

Capturing in the Corners

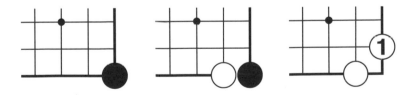

How many liberties does the Black stone have in the diagram on the left? You are right if you say, "two." In the middle diagram, if a White stone is next to the Black one, Black has only one liberty (and White has two). White can take with W1.

As you will see when you play your first few games, the characteristics of the sides and corners will create some very interesting situations.

Capturing in the Middle of the Board

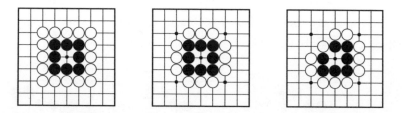

With these hypothetical shapes, what is going on? The White stones in the left diagram are *connected* along the straight lines, the ones on the right are not—but they are *virtually connected*. And they are cutting off Black's liberties.

In these three diagrams, Black is in atari with only one *internal liberty*—commonly called an *eye* in Go. Loosely defined, eyes are empty spaces surrounded by stones. This concept will become clearer as the professional game progresses.

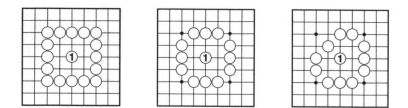

In these three cases, W1 would take the group. This is a concept that beginners sometimes find confusing, but it is easy if you think of Go as "hand talk"—one of the nicknames the ancient Chinese used for Go. First one player "signs," then the other. If it is your turn, you can "talk."

A Review of Capturing

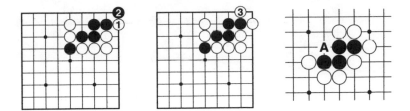

In this situation, why is B2 a wasted move? White will simply take with W3. How many liberties does the Black group of four stones have left? In other words, how many moves will it take White to capture Black? Two.

If this same group were in the middle of the board, and White took the four stones by playing at *A*, how many territory points would White also pick up? Four.

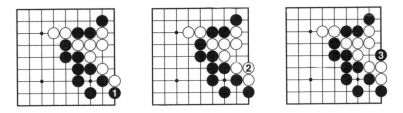

Here, B1 puts a White stone into atari. How can White defend? After W2 defends, how can Black put White into atari again?

B3 puts the lower three White stones into atari. After B3, how many liberties will each White group on the board have? The two stones on the upper left have four liberties, the group on the top right has three, and the group that is in atari has one.

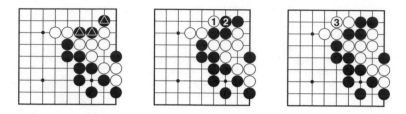

How many liberties do the marked Black stones at the top have? Before you answer, take a close look and calculate how many moves White would have to make before capturing them. The answers are not easy. White must protect, so Black still has three liberties.

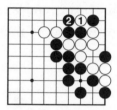
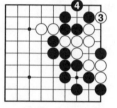
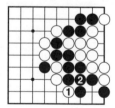

Either way, it is tough to kill Black. This situation will be explored in detail when the professional game reaches that point of play.

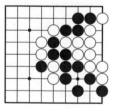
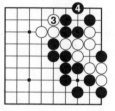
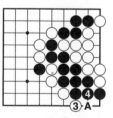

Suppose White was somehow able to magically surround Black. If it is White's move, this is how the capture would take place. A White stone at *A* would put Black into atari and Black could not avoid being taken.

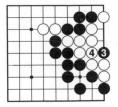

Black and White are now in a *capturing race*. After B3–W4, how many liberties does the Black group at the top have? How many does the White group have left? Is White in any danger? How about Black? The answer is tricky.

It seems like White has two liberties and Black has three at the top. But who will win the capturing race is hard to tell, as you will see by playing it out now or looking at the next few chapters.

The Capturing Game

To get used to playing on the intersections and taking pieces by surrounding them, you should play a few *capturer games*, in which the first person to take a stone is declared the winner.

It would seem that the next reasonable step would be to play some games where the winner is the one who can take the most stones. However, if you try this, or if you start playing Igowin in the AGA CD-ROM in the back of the book, some very confusing situations will arise. These will involve internal eyes and other types of empty spaces within the groups, among other things.

This is how real Go probably developed—people just started playing—but getting things figured out in a logical fashion must have taken them centuries, and, for you, it will certainly consume many frustrating hours, if not days.

Styles of Go playing will also cause some confusion. One of the intriguing things you will discover, for example, is that you will lose most of your games if killing is all you think about. You will find you need to think of *full-board strategies* involving not only the stones that are already on the board, but also empty areas where there are no stones. You will then see why you usually can't win everything on the board, and how the role of artful sacrifice is so important in Go and so absent in the capture game. Go is called the "supreme game of harmony and balance" because you must "give" to "get." After you play a few capture games, browse through the next few chapters—at least until chapter 6. If you are playing Igowin on the AGA CD-ROM, you might also want to look at the appendix on playing handicap Go. This way, you will see the game truly come "alive." You will see why the winners in Go are not the ones who are best at "killing," but the ones who are best at "living"!

CHAPTER THREE

All about Ladders

Like learning a language, in Go, reviewing makes perfect. Before continuing and learning about two new concepts, *double ataris* and *ladders*, ask yourself what has happened so far in the professional game.

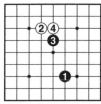 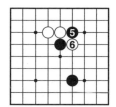 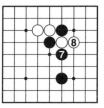

After the approach, extension, and block, White was almost surrounded and decided to run. Now the stones are splitting up and starting to grow into *groups*. It will help if you take the trouble to lay the game out on a board at this point because larger-scale consequences of the capturing rule are about to appear. They may be confusing at first, but you will soon be instantly recognizing them and knowing what to do about them as they come up in your games.

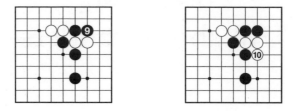

Black is chasing White. What would you do? There are many choices, of course. On the Go board, you are pretty much free to play wherever you want. W10 is a good move because it puts Black into danger. Before looking at the moves that follow, ask yourself, "Why?"

Double Atari

You can put a stone into atari when you make a move that leaves it with only one liberty. A double atari results when you put two stones into atari with one move. This is a very desirable or undesirable outcome, depending on whether it's happening to you or against you!

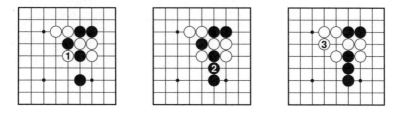

In the game, White is *threatening* to play W1, creating a double atari, where two stones are threatened. If Black tried to defend with B2, White could take the other Black stone. Go players would then say that White has one *strong group* and Black is split into two *weak groups*. White would be *dominating the board* and Black would be put on the defensive.

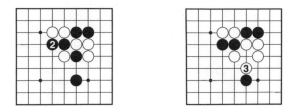

If Black defended the other way, it would be almost as bad! If you cannot understand this quite yet, please read a few more chapters. Once you grasp the ideas of territory and living groups, you will understand why Black would be at a disadvantage in this situation, and how easy it will be for White to win the game.

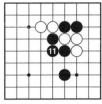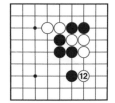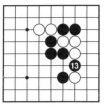

So, in the game, Black *protects*. Now both sides have two small groups that will be contesting each other. But they are not trying to capture just one or two stones. The players are using *whole-board thinking*.

White extends to W12. Ask yourself, "What are the players thinking about? What is the overall situation?" White seems to want the right side and Black the left. The top is up for grabs.

B13 threatens to *cut through* White and set up a *ladder*. Let's see what this means.

The Ladder

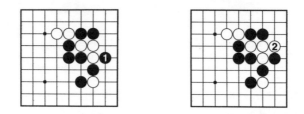

If Black could play B1, and if White tried to run . . .

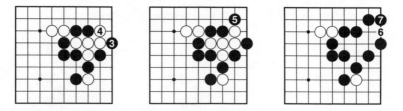

White would be *driven* to the edge of the board and would die. This is called *setting up a ladder* because the effect for White is like descending (or climbing) one step-by-step, stone by stone. White could try to walk down the steps but there would be no escape. This is one result. In the middle diagram, White would still be in atari and could be taken on the next move. W6 would be to no avail—Black would take with B7. If this happened, White would lose too many points and Black would win the game.

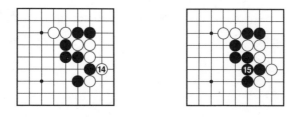

To avoid the problem, White puts Black into atari. So Black naturally protects.

At this point White seems to be stronger on the right side while Black has gained influence toward the lower left. Now, the players must take time to think about which parts of the board are *settled* with only the potential for small moves, and where there are opportunities to make bigger moves.

While they are thinking, please take some time to consider how double ataris and the clever use of ladders are two of the many components of the game that arise from the principle of surrounding. In the exercises below and in next chapter, you will see the ladder principle expanding over larger portions of the board. Soon ladders and awareness of them will be appearing in your games!

Some Ladder Exercises

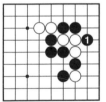

What if Black plays the other way to put White into atari? Try to work this out without putting stones down on a board.

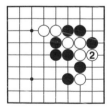
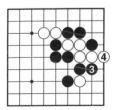
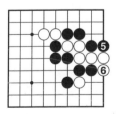

Black can take whether White plays W6 or not.

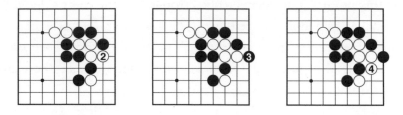

What if Black plays B3? This might look like a mistake, especially when W4 puts Black into atari!

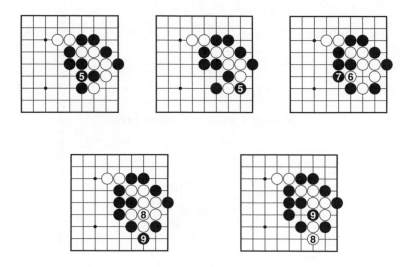

The simple way for Black to respond is to *fill*, but a more interesting way is to play B5 to keep White in atari.

White must take with W6, but B7 is the answer.

If White fills, B9 is the crushing move. And what if White doesn't fill? The only move is to extend down, but this doesn't look very promising since White is back in atari and can be taken on the next move, no matter what White does. This situation will be discussed a little later. But first, there will be an introduction to a vital aspect of ladders that, by now, you might be aware of and have questions about.

CHAPTER FOUR

Ladder Breakers, Loose Ladders, and Nets

If ladders exist in Go, then why not have ladder breakers? A *ladder breaker* is a stone that will save a group that is caught in a ladder. However, there are devices that can be employed to thwart ladder breakers. This is how the game of Go "goes." Strategies provoke counterstrategies that provoke even deeper strategies.

Ladder Breakers

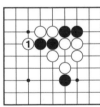 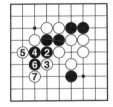 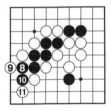

In this situation, if W1 starts a ladder, Black is, of course, dead. The characteristic form of the ladder should now be more obvious.

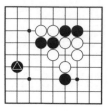

However, look at this hypothetical situation where Black has the marked stone in the lower-left corner.

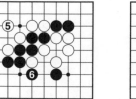

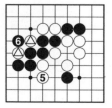

This is a variation of the ladder breaker in action. Black *links up*. White is now vulnerable at three places, *A*, *B*, and *C*.

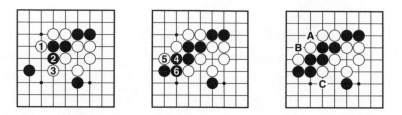

Black does well locally but may lose the game because the marked stones are vulnerable.

If White defends the other way, Black can double atari the marked stones and will probably win. For practice, see if you can find other ways for Black to capture and get a better or worse *outcome*! Also, try to find the ladder if Black doesn't defend after B8 in the middle diagram.

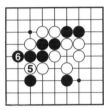 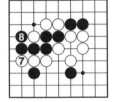 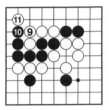

Is the marked stone a ladder breaker? If White falls asleep and plays W5, it is. B6 *connects* and Black escapes.

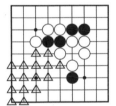

This W5 is correct. Black will not escape.

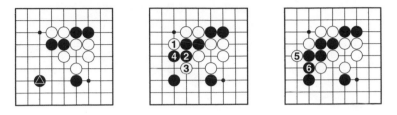

In general, care should be taken to *read ahead*, before starting a ladder with stones next to or in any of the marked areas.

Nets and Loose Ladders

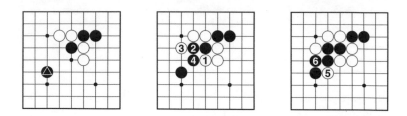

White has a problem. The marked stone seems to be an effective ladder breaker.

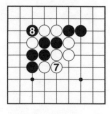
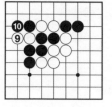
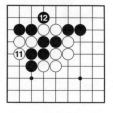

If White tries W7, disaster results. B12 starts a new ladder. If White played there first, White would be captured on the left side.

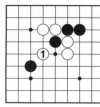
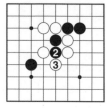
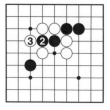

The *clever move* is to make a *net* that will trap the Black stone. Any Black move results in atari.

In this situation along the edge, if defending is the biggest move on the board, there are two proper moves for Black.

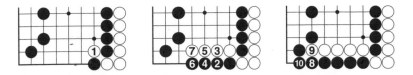

If White doesn't play cleverly, ordinary moves to capture Black will not work. Instead, it is White who will be captured.

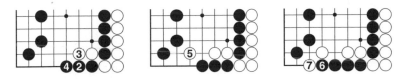

At this point, the proper move is to cast a net over Black. Black cannot escape.

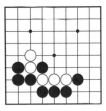

This classic problem should be easy to solve by now. How should Black play to capture?

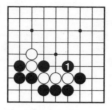

White cannot escape if it is Black's move.

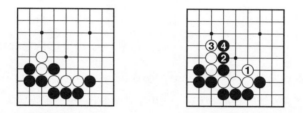

But what if it is White's move? W1 is one way, but the outcome is unsure. Is there a more *elegant* or *stylish* solution?

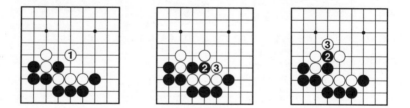

The good move is W1. Either way Black runs, there is no hope. This is the net in action.

The best way to learn about ladders and their relatives is to simply put some stones out on the board and try to capture them. You will be amazed at how ladders can sometimes bounce off the sides and how seemingly irrelevant stones can become the heroes or villains of your games.

CHAPTER FIVE

Clever Moves

Clever moves that are not obvious are called *tesuji* in Japanese. We saw one at the end of the last chapter. Of course, there are many levels of what is obvious. Nevertheless, tesujis have a certain beauty that places them apart from ordinary moves, as you will also see after a quick review of how the game stands so far.

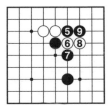
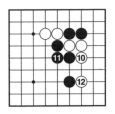
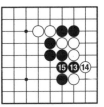

White's group was in danger and ran away. Then Black protected and White extended. There was danger of a ladder forming. Next, White avoided the ladder by putting Black into atari, and Black protected. The overall result was that White established influence on the right side and Black on the lower left. It is unclear what is going on at the top.

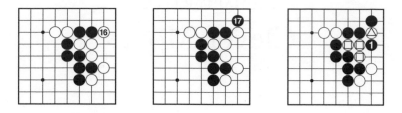

White is vulnerable. The best moves in Go are those with more than one meaning. W16 both defends the White group and attacks the two Black stones at the top.

It looks like Black is trying to defend the upper stones with B17.

If Black gets to play B1, it would be a double atari. The single stone marked with a triangle or the group of three stones marked with squares could be taken. Either result would be devastating for White and probably end the game.

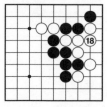
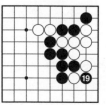
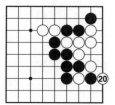

So White protects. Black next takes advantage of an opportunity and ataris White's stone at the bottom. White ataris back. But you might think that White is in trouble if you remember the exercises on pages 29–31.

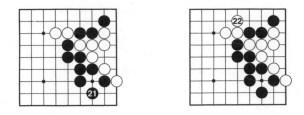

Black is *forced* to take and has made a few points. Black now controls the bottom and it's White's move. So White makes a high-level move at the top. If Black does nothing, what will happen to the two Black stones?

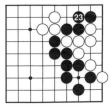 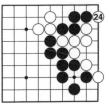 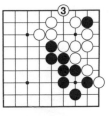

There will be no way out for Black. W1 is a tesuji.

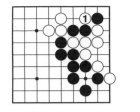 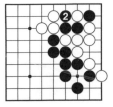

So Black protects. White responds to reduce the number of Black liberties. Now it looks like White might be able to surround Black first because Black now has only three liberties. But there is more to this than meets the eye, as you will see after some tesuji exercises.

Some Tesuji Exercises

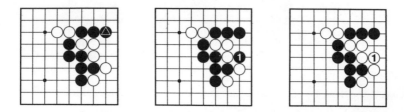

Earlier in the game, what was threatened if Black were able to play the marked stone? The tesuji would leave no escape, whether W2 was played or not. To avoid a collapse, White could try W1. What would Black's natural response be?

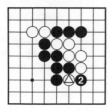
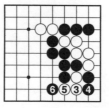
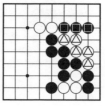

The atari of B2 is natural—it reduces White's liberties and is *profitable* because it secures territory at the bottom. A small ladder is involved if White tries to run away. Black can capture on the bottom at any time. The marked White stones have three liberties, and the marked Black stones have five. There is no question that White would lose everything.

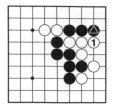

A different tesuji would have been involved if W1 were played. Try to visualize the sequence. You should be noticing the beginning of your abilities to do this.

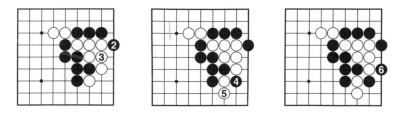

There would be no escape. This is why White played W16 in the game. Often the best play is where your opponent would like to play.

Another clever tesuji that all Go players know and love is the *monkey jump*. Imagine a monkey swinging from a tree branch and you will get the idea.

There are many lines of play to create and defend against monkey jumps that depend on the circumstances and whether one wants to keep the *initiative* to move elsewhere after it is finished. Here are some monkey jump examples along with several other tesujis from a brilliant game that will appear later in the book. However, this is only a brief taste and you should try working out some made-up problems yourself.

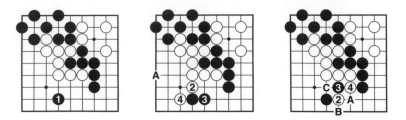

In this professional game from the advanced section, Black would like to monkey jump to B1. W2 is often the best defense, but W4 is too weak after Black *draws back* with the powerful B3. White's territory would be decimated. W2 at W4 is also useless.

Instead, the tesuji of W2 does the trick. If Black tries B3, the atari of W4 is devastating. If Black then tries *A*, White plays a *descending tesuji* at *B* and captures it. *C* is no good, either—White can surround and kill one of Black's two weak groups.

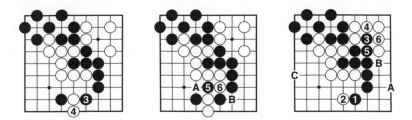

A desperate Black might try a *clamping tesuji* but another descending tesuji means that White can take at either *A* or *B*.

Therefore, in the game, Black will have to make the short jump of B1. White must block with W2 so Black keeps the initiative to make the forcing moves in the upper-right.

Next, Black will block at *B* to seal off the right side and prevent White from monkey jumping to *A*. The left side is still open for a Black monkey jump to *C*, or even worse, for an *invasion* but the meaning of all this must remain mysterious until the next chapter. This is where the seemingly dark business of killing will be replaced by the magical concept of living, gaining territory, and winning games!

PART TWO

The Middle Game and the Strategies of Go

We have already left the opening game, where the initial groupings that will influence the rest of game were set up. This is the middle game. As Richard Bozulich, Kiseido Publications' prolific writer, editor, and publisher, so succinctly put it:

> Of the three main stages in a game of Go, there is no doubt that the middle game is the most exciting. This is where most of the action of a game occurs: groups are attacked, defended or captured; potential territories are made, invaded or erased; game deciding, nerve-wracking *ko fights* and kill-or-be-killed capturing races take place. . . .

The next four chapters will cover all of these mysterious topics.

CHAPTER SIX

Life with Two Eyes and Thinking Territorially

The first chapter of this book introduced the basic idea of surrounding stones, and the next few showed some of the ways of capturing them. But if you can capture stones in Go, why can't you also capture empty intersections? This chapter will show how surrounding empty spaces in the right way can in fact prevent the resulting groups of stones from being captured. More than that, you will see how those groups can be skillfully used to capture even more stones and empty spaces and how Go ultimately becomes a game of who can control the most territory.

Let's go back to the idea of internal liberties, that is, unoccupied intersections that are surrounded by stones.

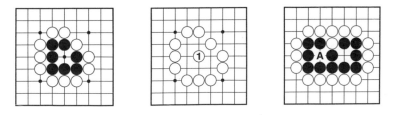

In these demonstration diagrams, White can take the Black group, even though it looks like W1 is surrounded by Black at first. But what happens if there are two internal eyes?

Can White play at *A*? Think about this for a minute before you look at the answer. What would happen, given the surrounding principle of Go? We know that Go is the most logical of games.

A would be a non-move for White—it would be meaningless and White would simply lose a move because Black still has one liberty left. So why bother making it?

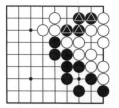

In the game, let's suppose White was given a few extra moves on the right side. For the sake of illustration, this might be one result. White would have two internal eyes and would be alive. In another way of saying it, the group could not be killed because Black cannot make two moves at the same time.

White would control two points of territory because of the two eyes, but what are the further consequences of having a living group and why are they important?

The second White group at the top is safe (it has five liberties to Black's three), so White would have virtually captured the marked Black stones. White would also gain the points of territory that they are occupying along with the empty intersections on the edge. Furthermore, White can also expand along the top. At this point, White could count on having 9 or 10 points of solid territory at the top, plus the 4 prisoners for a total of at least 13 or 14 points in that area.

The idea that White could expand is an important key to learning how to amass territory and win games of Go. This is because any stones or groups that are connected or virtually connected to a living group are also alive.

Thus, in this hypothetical position (remember, White was given extra stones), White would have a lot of influence across the top of the board that should turn into more points. Whether this would be enough to counterbalance Black's enormous amount of influence in the area below would not be clear until more moves are made. Let's see what this means.

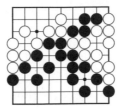

Jumping ahead, suppose, in this imaginary continuation, White was able to use the influence of the solid group to gain territory on the left.

As demonstrated in the introduction, Go games end when all the White and Black stones are joined up against each other and there are no plays left and no empty spaces in between. Neither Black nor White can play inside of each other's territory because there is not enough room to make a living group with two eyes. Any stones played there would die.

If the end of the game is in doubt, players should play things out until both sides think there are no more moves and both *pass*. Remember, it costs nothing to experiment as long as each move is answered. One player's stones would be dying, but the other player's stones would be filling in territory that has already been made.

Lastly, if one person keeps playing, then the game will continue, even if the other person continues to pass.

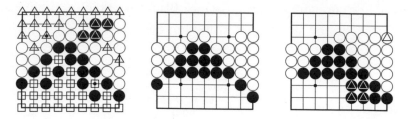

White's territory would include the area marked by triangles and Black's by squares.

The marked Black prisoners are then put into Black's territory and the result can be rearranged for easy counting.

In this case, White would have 23 points of territory plus 4 prisoners for a total of 27. Black would have 23 points and 1 prisoner. Note that because the prisoners are put into the opponent's territory, the result as laid out on the board looks different from the count—but the difference between the two players' scores remains the same. (In China the rules are slightly different—see the glossary entry for "Wei qi.")

Black is traditionally the weaker player and always plays first, except in handicap Go. However, if the players are evenly matched, Black gives up what is called *komi* for going first. In professional games, this is $6 \frac{1}{2}$ points. The half point means that there will be no ties, at least under ordinary circumstances.

So, White would have won this game by $9 \frac{1}{2}$ points.

Unfortunately, in the real game, White's influence had little effect and Black's was fully used, so the outcome was completely different. You will see why this happened in the next few chapters and the contrast will be enlightening. But first, let's examine the idea of double eyes in detail.

Understanding Eyes

Now that we can see what living groups with two eyes can do, let's look at some of the details of *eye shapes*—what makes them strong, what makes them vulnerable, and how you can use them. Knowing about the different types of eyes will allow you to read out positions and really understand what is going on beneath the surface in Go.

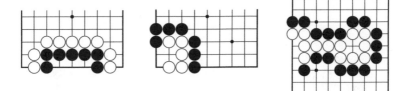

What needs to be done to these three shapes to make them alive? If it is the other player's move, what can be done to kill them?

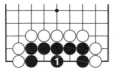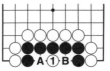

Black saves the group by playing B1. White can kill it by playing W1. A follow-up move (or a move by Black) at *A* or *B* would put the group into atari.

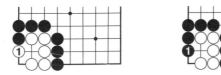

Similarly, W1 makes this corner shape alive; B1 kills it.

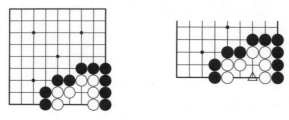

A three-space shape needs a move to make it alive or dead. The marked intersection is called the *vital spot*. A Black stone there will kill it. A White stone will make it alive.

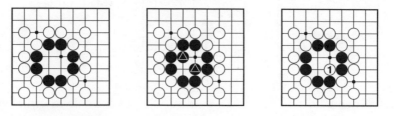

This four-space shape will need two moves to make it alive, but one move can kill it—if W1 is played, Black cannot make two eyes.

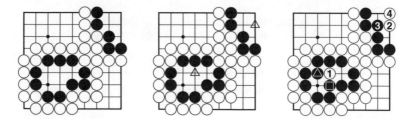

Five-space groups like these are vulnerable, too, at the marked spots. Again, where the opponent wants to play is often where you want to play.

Note that if Black could somehow get the two marked moves into the group in the middle diagram, there would be two eyes and it would be alive. W1 would of course be a wasted move. However, the method for killing the group in the corner with W2–W4 is simple, direct, and swift. There is nothing that Black can do.

This shape is called the *flower shape* in Japan and the *rabbity-six* in the West, since it looks somewhat like a rabbit with two long ears. It can be easily killed, as long as the correct moves are made.

After B2, if Black can get a move on the marked spot, the group will have two eyes and be alive. So White goes there first. The death struggle doesn't take very long. B6 makes it a three-space group that can be killed with W7.

To get a feel for life and death, lay out some stones and experiment. For example, try to find a four-space group that is alive. (If you can't, see page 81.)

False Eyes

By now, what constitutes an *eye shape* should be clear. However, there are many traps for the unwary. Sometimes, what seems to be an eye turns out to be a *false eye*—one that can be taken away. For beginners, this can cause some surprises.

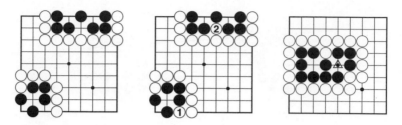

White's moves make these eyes false. White can take at any time because Black is in atari. Similarly, the group in the right diagram will die with a move at the marked spot.

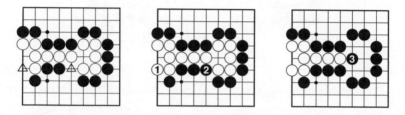

Here is a trickier situation. White will die because the marked spots are called points of *miai*—if White tries to make one eye, Black can make the second eye false. If W1 is at B2 making one eye, Black will play at W1.

The simple concept of living with two eyes and then being able to acquire territory is what makes the game of Go so intriguing and so complex. This is why professionals say that if you are going to "study" Go, solving life-and-death problems is the most beneficial for improvement. To satisfy that urge, there are hundreds of books with thousands of problems that can be studied for years. However, it is not recommended that you take that approach until much later in your Go career. The best thing at the moment is just to be aware of how the idea of surrounding stones and empty space leads to eyes and living groups, and ultimately territory.

By doing this, another concept you will become acquainted with is what constitutes *good* and *bad shape*. To encourage you to let your eyes do the reasoning, below are some examples of good and bad shapes that will be appearing as the book progresses.

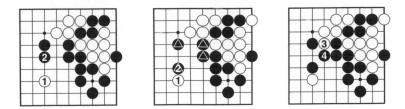

B2 has made what is called the *bamboo shape*. It is useful because it cannot be cut through. The second B2 is also good.

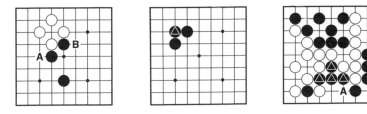

The shape of the marked stones means White will be alive.

On the right, a Black stone at *A* makes the valuable *mouth shape* which can trap the White stone.

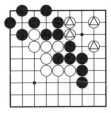
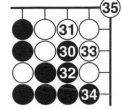
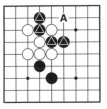

Another prized shape is the *ponnuki* whose influence extends over much of the board. Here, moves at *A* or *B* are threatened.

Lastly are two examples of bad shape. The first is the *empty triangle*. The marked stone contributes nothing and is redundant and the four marked stones are vulnerable at *A*.

CHAPTER SEVEN

Dead or Alive?

After you have been playing for a while you will see that being able to recognize *live* and *dead shapes* before your stones have been captured is a very important part of Go playing.

Live and Dead Shapes

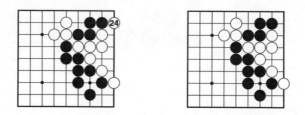

Remember how White played W24? Why was this done? What would happen if it wasn't played? Thinking about the life-and-death issues of the last chapter and on pages 29–31, see if you can spot the vital point in White's shape.

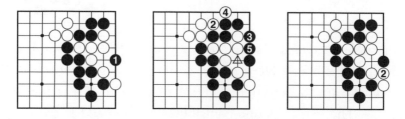

After B1–B5, playing on the marked spot is no good.

Neither is W2 as demonstrated on page 29.

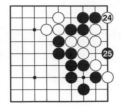

So White must play W24 to reduce the number of liberties of the Black group to three. Black still plays at the vital spot. What does this mean? As the next few pages will demonstrate, White is going to have to make plays to capture the four Black stones in order to make a living shape—the main groups cannot make two eyes even if Black didn't play B25.

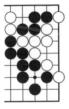 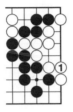 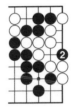

This is mainly a demonstration of living and dead shapes, so let's concentrate on the right side. W1 is not a good choice. B2 hits the vital spot.

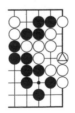

But what if White got to play the marked stone, too? Is it possible to make two eyes now?

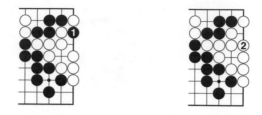

The *throw-in* of B1 would make the second eye false. It is called a throw-in because Black will lose the stone but this makes the second eye false.

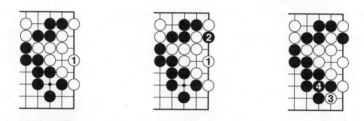

Suppose White tries W1 and Black makes the upper eye false. Can W3 be played?

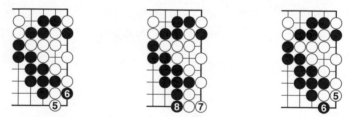

No. Black can make the bottom eye false with another throw-in. White is in atari and W5 on the right doesn't work either. Therefore, does White have a problem? We will return to that question after looking at a few other basic life and death problems.

Some Examples of Life and Death

Recognizing live and dead shapes takes practice. Work through these problems to help see how life and death works in different ways on the board.

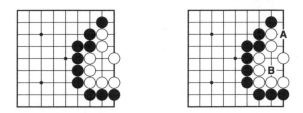

Can Black kill White? No, points *A* and *B* are miai—if Black plays at one, White can play at the other.

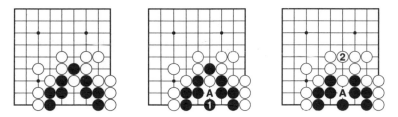

Can Black live? After B1, White cannot kill Black. White cannot play at *A* because it would be *suicide*. Suicides are prohibited under Japanese rules—they are considered non-moves. White must take, but after W2, White still cannot play at *A* without being taken. Black has two solid eyes.

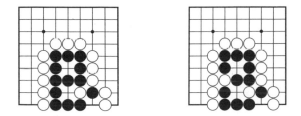

Can Black live in both of these situations? Look at them carefully.

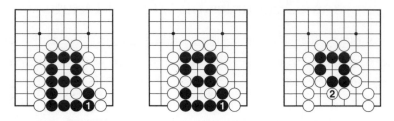

Black is alive in the first example, but B1 in the second is self-atari and White would be able to take on the next move.

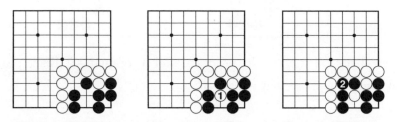

Can White kill Black? Again, you must study the situation. With the throw-in of W1, Black is helpless. Black cannot play B2 in the second diagram because it is self-atari. White can take on the next move.

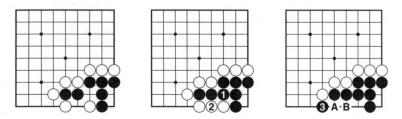

This is a famous problem. If it is White's move, it is easy to kill Black. But if it's Black's move, what can be done to save it? B1 saves the group. If White resists, Black can make an eye by playing at *A* or *B*.

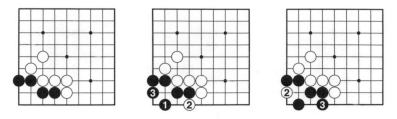

Black is to play and live. B1 is the key move. White cannot kill with either W2.

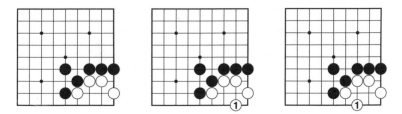

Which is the correct way for White to live?

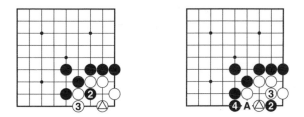

In the first diagram the marked stone is the right move. Black can do nothing because of White's shortage of liberties.

If the marked White stone in the second diagram is played, B4 kills the group because White cannot play at *A*. It would be self-atari. Black can play at *A* to kill the group if White takes B2.

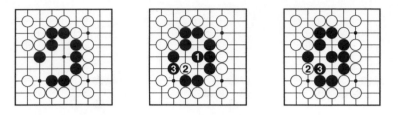

Can Black live by playing properly? This is a difficult problem! Either B3 gives Black life.

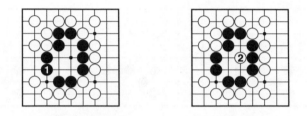

However, a misplay results in one of the classic five-space shapes that can be killed with one move.

Live Groups in the Corners, Sides, and Center

It is much easier to make eyes and territory in the corners and on the sides of the board. It is like having extra stones at your disposal. These final examples will help demonstrate why.

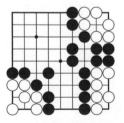

Six stones are needed to form the smallest two-eyed groups on the corners.

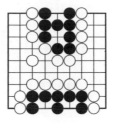

Eight or nine are needed on the sides.

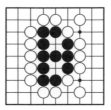

And eleven stones are required to make a two-eyed group in the middle.

Because of these "geometric" considerations, in big-board Go, play generally starts in the corners. The first person to play there has a big advantage and eyes are easy to make. Because of these factors, one feels safer in next making aggressive or extending moves along the sides, which generally become the second object of attention. Then, usually—but not always—play ventures into the uncharted areas of the center.

To get used to these ideas, most of the games presented in this book begin near the corners or on the sides. However, there has been much experimentation carried out on playing in the center for the first move on boards of all sizes. This tactic will be discussed later in the book.

Next, however, another vital aspect of Go needs to be explored. Because B25 in the game was not meant to deprive White of eyes, you will learn why it was purely a *fighting move* that takes advantage of White's vulnerable shape.

CHAPTER EIGHT

Running Fights in Sente and Gote

If the surrounding principle creates the "body" of Go, then the ebbing and flowing of *sente* and *gote* is like its heartbeat. More than just moves, sente and gote represent the pulsing energy of the game. To put things simply, sente is when you are on the offensive and gote is when you are on the defensive. Sente is when you have the initiative—your opponent feels he or she must answer your move. Gote is when there is no response to your move and a play is made on another part of the board. To see this more clearly, a few more moves in the game will be looked at and then a review will take place.

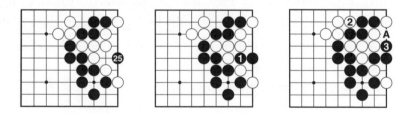

We know that B25 was not meant to deprive White of eyes, so why did Black move there? If Black could play B1 next, it would be fatal for White. In the capturing race that would follow, the five White stones above it would only have two liberties and the Black stones on top of them would have three. After B3, White seems to have two liberties but cannot play at *A* because of self-atari.

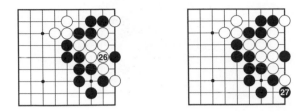

So White must play W26 to defend. This means that B25 was a *forcing move*—one that White had to answer. B27 attacks while sealing off territory at the bottom—the best kind of move. It also gives Black solid eye shape, meaning that Black no longer has to worry about an attack coming from the left side. The White group now has only three liberties, plus there is a volatile situation at the top.

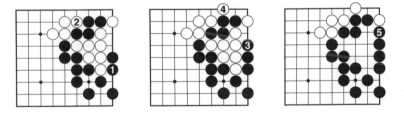

If it was Black's move, there would be nothing that White could do after the B3–W4 exchange, both White and Black would have only one liberty, but it would be Black's turn to take with B5.

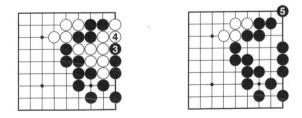

If White played at W4, as in this diagram, it wouldn't work, either. W4 would put the three Black stones on the right side into atari, but Black could take with B5.

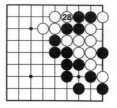

So White must play W28 in gote to reduce Black's liberties to two. In other words, Black has sacrificed the four stones at the top in order to keep White hemmed in and on the defensive. As you will see a number of other times in the book, sacrifices of something small are used to keep sente and gain something big in the future. This is a very big part of Go strategy. So far in this game, Black has mostly kept sente. The reasons for this are not easy to see.

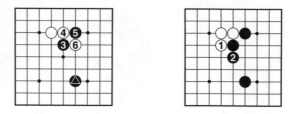

In the cold light of post-game analysis, the decision at the beginning of the game to cut with W6 was fatal because Black could coordinate an attack in sente by using the presence of the bottom marked stone that was Black's first move. White had little choice. If W1 was played, for example, Black would be playing on the center line and be gaining too much territory. The real culprit is the direction of play of B4. It makes the blocking move of W5 too natural of a response. Blocking moves like this are called *hane* in Japanese. What White should have done will be explained later in the book. But even after this mistake, Black had to play expertly to take full advantage of White's weakness. It required an early decision to sacrifice.

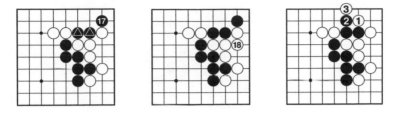

It was B17—which was also a forcing move—that made this sacrifice of the two marked stones bigger and more effective. It also made Black's encirclement of White so relentless. Sacrificing is such an important part of Go, a whole chapter will be devoted to it. If B17 were not played, White could have taken the two Black stones at any time in a ladder.

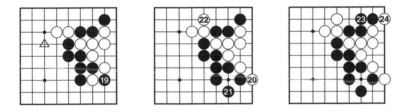

Black's next move ended in gote, but it was important for two reasons and was well thought out. White would have loved to play at *A* to increase territory and reduce Black's, but, as was demonstrated, there would be a problem living on the right side.

White could do only one thing with sente, however—play the tesuji of W2—but that created more unavoidable problems. Black's response took back sente because of White's shortage of liberties. The four Black stones became a bitter poison pill that White had to swallow. Thus, the gote move of B19 allowed White to continue on in sente—making it a *sente no gote* move. This is a gote move that allows a sente move later on.

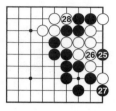

White had to continue *following orders* on the right side and answer each of Black's moves, because the group was too large to lose.

In the series of sente moves between B25 and W28, Black *took profit* in the lower-right corner, while White's defensive gote moves gained nothing on the right side. White also lost a point at the top by having to fill *inside territory*.

In addition, Black will eventually get two more sente moves in this area by taking the White stone above B27 and threatening to win the race to capture. The remaining sente move will force White to take the four Black stones and to fill in two more points of territory, as you will see later in the game. But there are other issues to settle before this that are worth many more points. And, as you will also see later on, there are some strategic reasons for not making these moves now.

Reverse and Double Sente

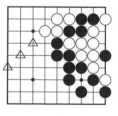 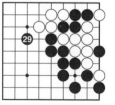 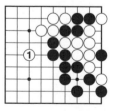

Whenever groups are contesting for territory, moves that increase one's own group while reducing the opponent's are twice as valuable. It is easy to see why, in this game, getting the first move into the marked area is going to be critical. B29 gains Black territory, makes White's smaller, and also keeps sente because it threatens to invade even more White territory in the top left.

Imagine the difference if White had been able to play W1! This would have been a sente move, too, because it would threaten to invade Black's territory. Thus, B29 is a sente move and also a *reverse sente* move, making it *double sente*. This is worth twice as much as the value of an ordinary sente move. What White would have gained must be added to what Black gains.

The general idea is to play sente moves until you can play a big gote move and take profit. Remember, however, that the value of a gote move will be diminished by the value of the opponent's next move. If that move is sente, the loss is even greater. The calculations about the value of moves in the back-and-forth of sente and gote can get complicated, but the rule of thumb is that gote moves are worth about half of sente moves.

Again, the game comes to a pause. While the players are considering what is happening *on the big board*—in other words, what has changed with Black getting to the upper left first with B29—we will look at two other aspects of Go that result from the surrounding principle. You may have come across them already in your games and noticed that they seem to interrupt the normal ebb and flow of sente and gote.

CHAPTER NINE

Ko and Seki

The surrounding principle of Go can produce two mystifying situations that you may have encountered already in your games.

Ko

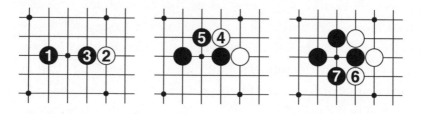

Suppose this sequence occurs in the opening of a beginners' game.

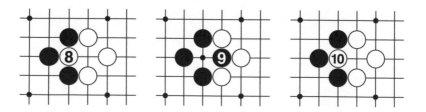

Can Black take back immediately? And then can White take back? No. This situation is called *ko*, which is taken from a Buddhist word for "eternity" because it is something that could go on for a long time. In the hand talk of Go (as in life), every move must have a unique meaning. If ko could go on forever, nothing would happen—there would be no change. So, because a board position cannot be repeated, a move somewhere else must be made before taking back the ko.

Ko Threats

Ideally, a *ko threat* is a move that threatens to take something bigger than whatever is at stake in the ko. It will cause the opponent to answer, at which point the ko can then be taken back because the board has changed from the original position. This back-and-forth process sometimes goes on for many moves, and the values of the countermoves decrease to the size of the ko, at which point one or the other player fills the ko. Of course, if a player has no ko threats, the biggest move will be played and the other player will fill the ko. This process will become clearer after looking at the examples below. A ko can be worth a lot or only a point in gote, as these examples from the edge and corner demonstrate.

In these two examples, if the ko is filled, and it affects nothing else, it will be a gote move that is worth less than a point.

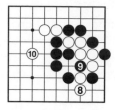

Remember this situation on page 38? White extended and Black took. But White's biggest threat was W10, which is not enough to deter Black from simply taking the group.

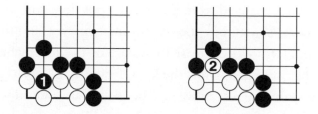

In this interesting situation in the corner, if Black plays B1, attempting to capture White, White can take back immediately if this position has not appeared in the game yet.

Black must play elsewhere and make a move that is worth more than the 15 points that the group is worth (6 stones and 7 points of territory—remember that Black must put down 2 stones to take the group and White will have 2 points of territory if the group lives). From this total, the value of the move that White can play afterwards must be subtracted because in this situation the group would be taken in gote.

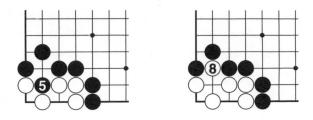

Next, if such a move is found and White answers, then Black can take back with B5. White finds a move that is worth the value of the group and can take back with W8.

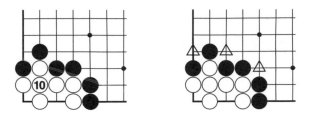

Let's suppose that the only move that Black can find is worth less than the ko—say 5 points. White then fills the ko with W10 to save the group, but then Black gets to move elsewhere—say a move worth 2 points. So White has made 15 points, but has lost 7 for a profit of 8. However, if the last Black move is sente, the value of the succeeding move or moves must also be factored in. This intertwining of mathematics and Go is interesting, and many professional Go players perhaps could have become mathematicians. On the other side of the fence, renowned combinatorial game theorist Elwyn Berlekamp, a 9-kyu, devised highly complex theorems that could beat 9-dan professionals in analyzing the descending values of the final points of some Go games. Needless to say, amateur Go players just approximate these numerical values.

Besides the math, the effect on the surrounding situation must be considered. In this case, Black is left with weaknesses at the marked spots, so whatever stones and territory are lost and which defensive moves are made must be put into the equation, too.

Unless the stakes are high and the game is extremely close, all that is absolutely necessary in this situation is to make a rough count, noting that it is in the corner and therefore worth more than it appears to be at first glance.

As you might guess, ko is an extremely important element of advanced Go playing, so don't worry if you encounter some mystifying situations in some of your games. The idea is to experiment freely, play boldly and not worry if you lose a few times. This is easy to do on 9 x 9 boards. Later in the book, there is a game that features a failed attempt to use ko to turn a loss into a victory, and another one where a ko strategy is used to keep sente and win.

Seki

Think of seki as something like an area of calm on the Go board, where nothing can happen—where there is no "energy" left to play. Because of the surrounding principle, it is where neither player wants to make a move since it would put one into self-atari. The surrounded territories involved in a seki count for nothing under Japanese rules. However, seki can sometimes be used to save an otherwise dead group, so along with ko, it can be used as another strategic weapon.

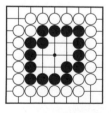

Remember the Black rabbity-six or flower shape and how it could be killed if it was White's move? What if it had one more internal liberty in the lower right to make it a seven-space group?

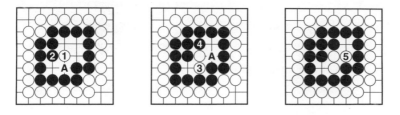

White starts out as before. This is the *center of symmetry* and is usually the logical place to start saving or killing groups. After W1–B2, if Black gets a stone at *A*, a second eye will result, so White would play there. After W3–B4, the same situation exists, so White plays W5. But now what will happen?

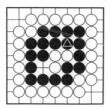
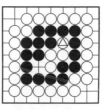

Black would not want to play the marked stone. It would be self-atari, and White could take on the next move. But White would not want to play there either. Why?

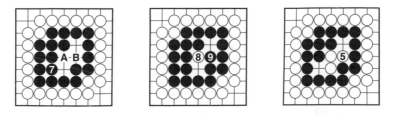

After B7, it becomes a four-space group that is automatically alive. *A* and *B* are points of miai—if White plays one, Black can play the other. After W8, Black plays B9, for example.

What would happen after W5? Neither side wants to play there. Black doesn't want to die and White, although winning, doesn't want to give up the 2 points of territory and 4 prisoners. White has forced a seki, but if this was on a bigger board, it would also be to Black's advantage because White ends in gote so Black could then move elsewhere.

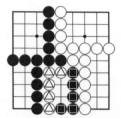

This is another example of seki. In this fanciful situation, can the marked stones ever be killed? No, because it would be suicidal for either player to try to take the other's stones.

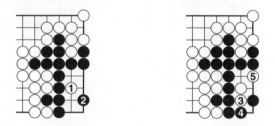

In this position, if Black fails to play at B2 first, W1 will create a seki. See if you can find other ways to create the seki, assuming Black cannot win a ko. If you can't at this point, try again later on because it appears in a game in the advanced section.

For now, it is good enough to just know that ko and seki situations can exist and what can be done about them, if anything. Just be aware that seki infrequently develops in capturing races between both eyeless and one-eyed groups, while, as mentioned, the much more important and frequent instances of ko will be the subject of a whole chapter later in the book.

PART THREE

The Endgame

The endgame is approaching. If the opening game was an opportunity for expressing the artistic, "left-brained" side of your mind, and the middle game was the time for sharpening your wits, then the endgame is the time to use the "bean counting" abilities of your "right brain."

The next two chapters will show you how differently beginners and professionals might look at the last stages of the game we have been following.

CHAPTER TEN

The Endgame I:
The Beginner's Way

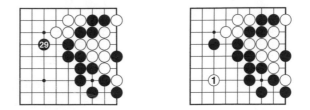

After taking advantage of keeping sente during the long struggle on the right side, Black can finally take the last big point of the game by playing B29. Not only is it big territorially, but if it keeps sente, meaning if White passively defends what is left of the possible territory on the upper side, then it becomes a double sente move, worth twice as much as an ordinary sente move.

Whether it keeps sente or not, B29 is so big that it puts Black ahead. Therefore, White must consider if it is an *overplay* and think about the possibilities of invading. Invasion will be the subject of the last chapter of the book, where it will be a kind of "graduating" exercise that will get you ready for big-board play. Needless to say, invading is always a delicate issue, and its success or failure can decide the outcome of a game in a matter of a few moves. In other words, could the bold move of W1 live?

Aji

Black would have to be careful because several intersections above this stone, *aji* is hovering. In Japanese, *aji* literally means "taste" (think of the *aji no moto* of Japan or the MSG of Chinese food). There is good aji and bad aji, depending on your point of view. Here, there is bad aji for Black, meaning Black is vulnerable.

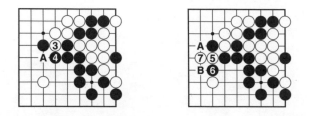

The aji would become apparent if Black was lax and played elsewhere. If White had the opportunity to push with W3, there is a weakness at *A*. After W5, Black would have to block at *B*. Blocking at *A* is worse because White could play at *B* and live with two eyes in the corner.

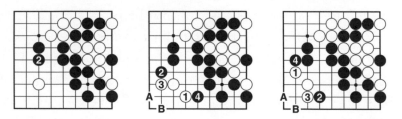

However, it is not White's move so Black can take care of the problem. One answer is to make the *bamboo shape* with B2. It is especially valuable because it cannot be "broken." That is, it cannot be *cut through*. At the end, the invading stone in the corner is dead. White would need stones at both *A* and *B* to live, but that is impossible.

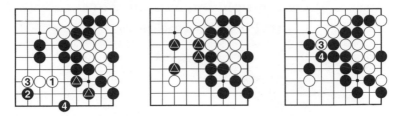

The third alternative doesn't work, either. Because of the power of the marked stones, Black can connect.

It does not necessarily hurt trying to make a group live like this because as long as the opponent answers, the score remains the same. However, in this case, Black would have become stronger on the left and White would lose the points that would have been gained by playing patiently. In other words, White will have to *reduce* instead of *invade* and hope for a blunder or a series of minor mistakes that will add up. All Go players learn how fast "small" can add up to "big" and that endgame oversights are common, especially when there are time constraints, as the "big ko" game in the advanced section will show. Players must think out their endgame moves very carefully!

Before reading any further, you should take some time to lay out the stones on a board or on an electronic one in the AGA CD. Then, by yourself or with a friend, try to play out the rest of the game, keeping in mind that Black must give up 6 $^1/_2$ points in komi. Write down the score, then reverse the colors and play it again. By doing this, you will find different *lines* of play and will also gain a better understanding of what the thinking is on the opposite side of the board. There is no faster way to become stronger because you will discover that what looks easy can often be very complex.

Two Simple but Wrong Ways
to Play the Endgame

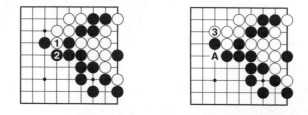

To prevent that unfavorable outcome after the *slack* move of W1, Black would have to respond, so W3 would seem to threaten *A*.

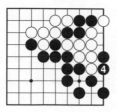 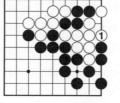 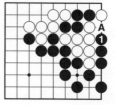

But Black would not have to respond immediately. B4 on the right side is sente. White cannot play at W1 in the middle diagram—it would be self-atari. And Black with B1 would be one move away from giving atari to the big White group. If White plays at *A*, the group is still in atari.

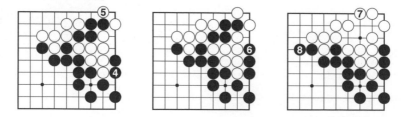

So, after B4, White must play W5. Following another push, White would have to take. Then Black could play B8 on the left side.

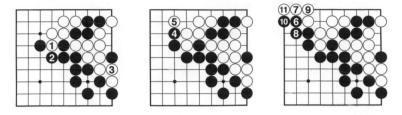

What if White played on the right side first? White would gain 4 points on the right and wouldn't have to use two stones to take the Black group, while Black would lose the stone that would otherwise have been taken. The value is about 6 points (depending on what happens in the top left), but it is gote, so the value of Black's next move must be factored in. That move is also big. However, if White plays like this, is there a trick move after W11? W11 seems like a *dame* point. Dame points are places at the end of a game that can be filled by either player and are worthless. But is that the case here? Endgames can sometimes be full of surprises as the dame are filled in!

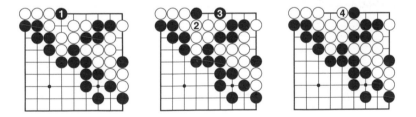

Be careful if you see a pattern like this in one of your games! B1 is in atari. If W4 took, White would still be in atari and Black could take the whole group.

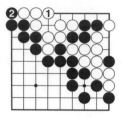

However, there is no problem. If W1 is played first, B2 fills the dame. But this reduces the value of the moves on the right by 1 point. Played this way, White would have 13 points of territory and 5 prisoners for a total of 18. Black would have 33 territory points and 1 prisoner. With the $6\frac{1}{2}$ point komi, Black would win by $9\frac{1}{2}$ points.

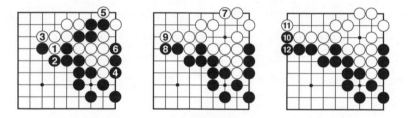

So, what happens if White obeys orders and plays the sequence like this?

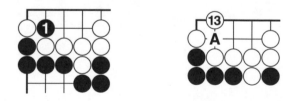

White must be careful in the corner. Often in the endgame, Go players forget to secure their *borders*—the areas between the contesting groups. White can play W13 but is subject to a ko threat at *A*, so defending solidly is often better.

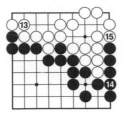

After W13, Black can also pass—give up a turn—and let White play W15 and then fill in at B14. It doesn't matter in the score who plays at these two points, although there is an atari involved. In this outcome, Black would have 30 points of territory plus 2 prisoners. White would have 13 points of territory plus 4 prisoners. With komi, Black would win by 8 $1/2$ points. This is a rather large difference in a professional 9 x 9 game and the players would have read out and rejected these two simple lines of play.

We have seen how an invasion can try to take advantage of aji. If, in the course of endgame skirmishing, you feel the situation might get out of hand, or if it is beyond your power to read the sequence out, always consider safety moves!

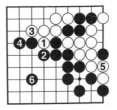

In this situation, think about how comfortable you might feel if you made a move on the *3-3 point*. However, a move like that would be played in gote, so White would gain far too much. As you will see in the next chapter, there is actually a volatile situation on the upper left that will require all of Black's resources, so the luxury of a move like B1 would never become an option.

CHAPTER ELEVEN

The Endgame II: The Professional Way

White would definitely not be interested in how the simple sequences came out. The game is lost because of the bad move early in the game, but professionals, after all, have reputations to maintain, and *fighting spirit* is the most admired quality of professional Go players. Also, as we will see in the last game of this book, as well as in your own games, there is always the possibility of a serious mistake popping up, especially in a fast game. And remember, too, about the lurking aji, and a rule of thumb in 9 x 9 Go that if White can manage to make two living groups, the game will usually be won because of komi—the points Black must give up for going first.

So the question is, how can White complicate things or at least cut down the loss and exit gracefully? As with most endgames, once the simple path is left, there are many variations to consider in great detail. Don't feel embarrassed if this chapter requires a number of readings to understand the main threads of thought. And, remember, also, that it is always easier when you lay the stones out on the board to follow events.

A Professional Endgame

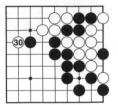

The tesuji of W30 helps White "muddy the waters" as the Chinese might put it. Now the question for Black is which side to play on.

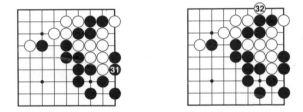

First comes B31, however. It is *absolute sente* that White, as demonstrated in the last chapter, must answer with W32. But why did Black waste a potentially valuable ko threat here? Go players are extremely careful not to waste threats in case there is an unforeseen ko that the opponent can set up. However, B31 is big because it prevents White from playing there first, as illustrated in the last chapter. Also, both players have read out the endgame and, in case of a mistake, Black still has another threat and White does not. You will understand more of this concept later in the chapter.

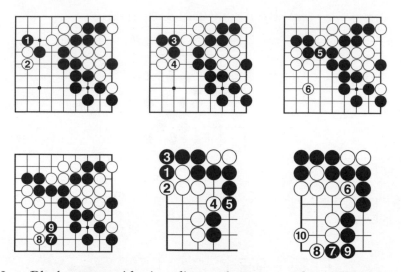

Now, Black can consider invading at the top to reduce White's territory. But Black would have a *cutting point* that must be defended with B3 so White could live with two eyes on the bottom. This is one way.

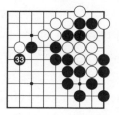

Since White cannot make any significant territory on the right side after the stone was taken by B31. Black plays B33, calculating that the win is a sure thing.

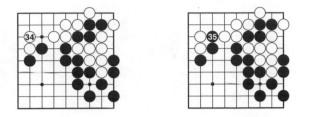

White must *draw back* with W34. This is an often-used, standard defensive move. Black follows up by pushing.

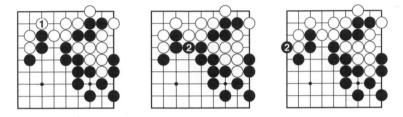

Should White block at W1?

Which B2 would be better?

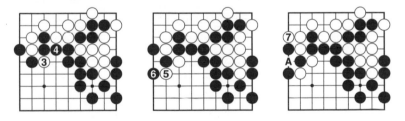

The first way would be disastrous for Black and a mistake that White would have been hoping for. White would not have to play ko at *A*. Instead, W7 finishes off Black. If Black filled, the three stones would be taken. If Black tried to run down the board, White would simply take two stones with a move at *A*.

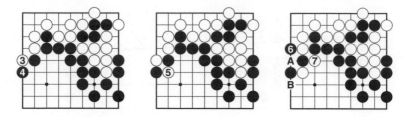

In this continuation, could Black play B4? W5 would create a double atari. This looks dangerous. Black could not prevent the ko by filling at *A*, since White *B* would put the three stones into atari.

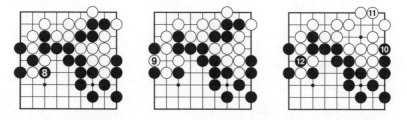

Black would play like this. It might look hopeful for White, but Black has a last ko threat! After White takes, Black could take back the ko. White has no threats that even come close to being this large.

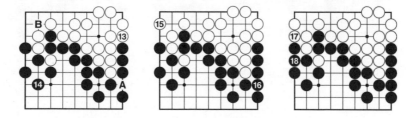

White could play W13, but there would only be a few points there. If White tried to take them with *A*, Black *B* would decimate the upper-left side. If this continuation was played the proper way, Black would have 26 points of territory and 4 prisoners while White would have 13 points on the board and 5 prisoners, which would total 18. Black would win by 5 $^1/_2$ points after komi.

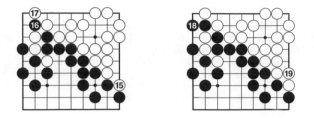

Just for exercise, what if White made a mistake and took in the lower-right? B18 is a descending tesuji that keeps points for Black in the corner (see pages 50 and 152 for other examples).

Played the other way, B18 prevents White from playing there after the capture.

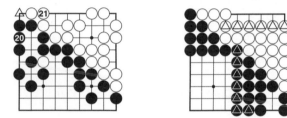

The dame is marked. Black would have 29 points of territory and 6 prisoners for a total of 35. White would have 11 territorial points and 7 prisoners for a total of 18. After komi, it would be a $10\,^1/_2$ point victory for Black.

Looking carefully at different results is good practice to develop a sense of what various moves are worth compared to each other. Again, because of the geometry of the board, taking roughly an equivalent number of stones in the corner is usually an automatically better move than taking them along the sides or in the center. This is because the opponent will have difficulties in approaching afterward. You will learn to do this almost automatically.

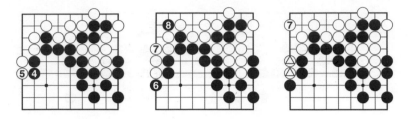

What if Black drew back and White followed? Then it would be a lesson for those who are afraid of ko!

B8 would be quite a surprise for White whose marked stones would have to be given up by making a move like W7 in the upper left.

Let's get back to the real game. White has a trick to save a point by keeping sente.

Continuing to the End

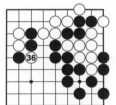
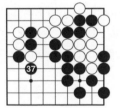
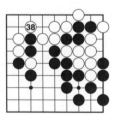

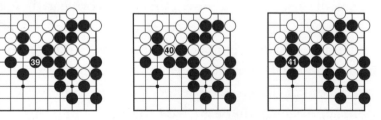

W36 is a sacrifice tesuji. This time it is Black that must swallow a poison pill! However, coming so late in the game, the profit is minuscule.

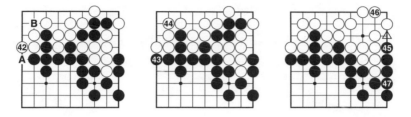

W42 might seem conservative, but it is the biggest move on the board. There is still the problem at *B* if White played at *A*. White must fill inside territory with W44.

Finally, Black pushes on the right side and White must take. Again, the marked point is a dame and it doesn't matter who fills it. However, to avoid confusion, the dames are usually filled in rotation. It is very important to remember that even professional players have lost games when dames result in unexpected ataris. Here, it is White's turn to fill the dame.

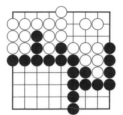

Filling in the prisoners and rearranging the stones so the territory appears in groups of five, Black has 26 points and 2 prisoners for a total of 28. White has 14 points and 4 prisoners for a total of 18. The real game ends with a victory for Black by 3 $^1/_2$ points. In a professional 9 x 9 game, this is a significant difference from the other results that were looked at.

A Review of the Game

A quick review reveals some of the highlights of this game.

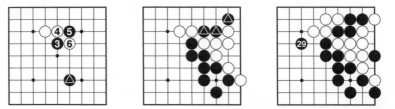

Cutting with W6 was fatal because of the position of the marked stone.

After being forced into a bad position by a series of sente moves, the marked Black stones are offered up for sacrifice. White must swallow the poison pill.

As shown in the chapter on sente and gote, B29 is the big double sente move that seals the victory. Black's lead is overwhelming for professional play because White cannot invade the lower left.

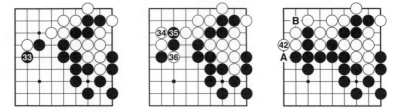

Next, Black makes the right choice by defending the territory instead of invading the upper left, even though the sequence ends in gote.

White cleverly sacrifices to gain momentum but then White must play W42 instead of at *A*, because Black could then play *B*. After Black responds by playing at *A*, White must play *B* in gote. White is then forced to take the four Black stones in the upper right, and the game is over.

During this long game, we hope you have become acquainted with the basic elements of good Go playing. It began with the capture of stones using ladders, tesujis, and sacrifices. Then it progressed to the idea of capturing empty intersections and making live groups with two eyes that can surround additional territory. It also showed how aji can hover in certain areas of the board and how ko and seki can affect the ebb and flow of gote and sente.

The next sections will greatly enlarge on some of these concepts and give some ideas on how they can be put to use in your games.

PART FOUR

Advancing in Go

The first game in this book covered most of the general concepts of Go playing, Now it is time to focus on specific strategies that will help prepare you for big-board play. The games of this section are highly unusual. They were chosen because they offer wonderful examples of how professionals use sacrifice, ko, cross-cuts, aji, tesujis, invasions, and the killing of large groups to further their ultimate aim of making territory. These advanced concepts are difficult to teach on larger boards, but they are easy and to the point when they are spotlighted within the smaller confines of the 9 x 9 size.

CHAPTER TWELVE

Harnessing the Powers of Sacrifice

You will find that as your ability to sacrifice—to not cling to every stone—increases, your progress in Go will increase. To sacrifice means to be able to see far enough ahead to give up something small (or a group in a hopeless condition) in exchange for getting something bigger later on. This is truly close to the heart of the game, and you will see why sacrificing can be called an art form of its own. In practical terms, sacrifices demonstrate the ancient Taoist goal of "gaining the most for the least amount of effort." When successfully employed, they can be objects of great beauty.

Sacrificial Maneuvering

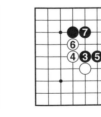 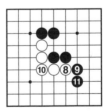

As we know by now, there is nothing unusual in the opening moves of this professional 9 x 9 game. The players calmly go about dividing up the board.

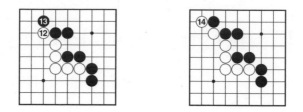

The fireworks begin. There is a Go proverb that says, "Hane at the head of two stones to block their progress." W12 is the hane. After B13, W14 is a *double hane* that is a challenge! The response to a double hane must be carefully considered because there are always many possibilities.

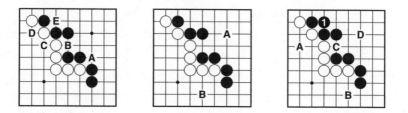

The first things to consider in a double hane like this are the vulnerable cutting and atari points created from *A–E* in the first diagram.

Next, what effects these sensitive points would have in the battle for the open areas around *A* and *B* must be considered. The goal for both players is to end with sente to move into those territorial areas first.

A simple response to the double hane is B1. White would then have to decide whether to defend at *A* or *B* and/or how a push at *C* would affect an attempt to live at *D*. These are complicated questions! Let's see what happened in the game.

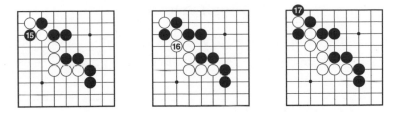

Black ataris twice.

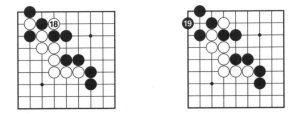

This *invites*, or rather forces, White to start sacrificing.

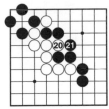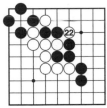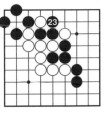

Next, White pushes and Black must block. W22 ataris. Again, Black must respond.

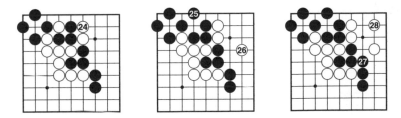

W24–W26 are also sente. Black must play B25–B27. W28 makes a familiar strong shape (see pages 61 and 87), which assures life.

A Bigger Sacrifice

Professional instincts for style will also be a factor in the following game, where an even bigger sacrifice will be made.

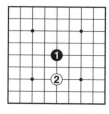
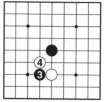
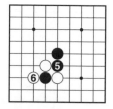

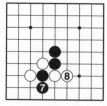
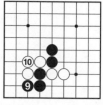
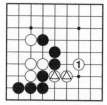

In this fast TV game, the fighting starts immediately. The players will be constantly calculating whether to save their groups or abandon them. After B7, White is going to force Black to swallow a sacrifice of the two White stones on the right. It is a *one-way street*. Black has no choice but to use B13 to lean on White. White has the possibility of making territory on the right side, but is *undercut* by Black, so it would not amount to much. White must make territory at the top to have a chance in this game. The problem presented for Black is that the marked stones can run at W1 and live. So . . .

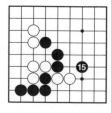
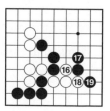
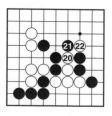

After B21, probably any beginning player would think of resigning, but actually it is all part of White's game-winning strategy that begins with W22.

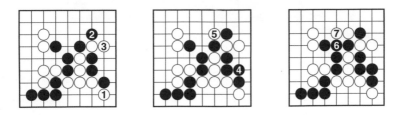

If White plays W1 and Black tries the atari of B2, it is clear that Black will lose the capturing race.

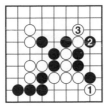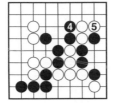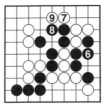

If Black ataris upward it is more complicated but the result is the same. Black cannot escape. If B4 is played at W5, White will play at B4 and also capture the center group.

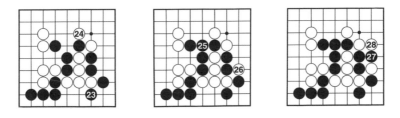

Black must play B23, so White attacks at the top. Black is forced to fill. Then, with W26, White starts another sacrifice.

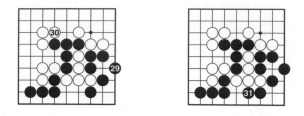

With seeming cruelty, White methodically forces Black to respond. After the capture of the throw-in stone, Black must keep the number of White liberties less than those of the center group.

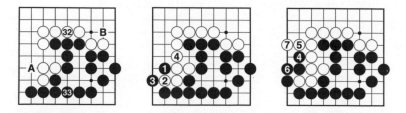

When Black is forced to capture in gote, White's plan is a complete success. White deliberately lost 12 points (10 in the big group plus the single stone and its territory), but gained the entire top of the board. Note, too, how Black's stones consumed at least six intersections of inside territory. Forcing the opponent to take like this will always create a favorable outcome.

Although the game is won no matter what Black does, White must decide which Black move would be the biggest to stop, A or B. The "easy" answer of B is shown above, but the tricky answer of A is better and will serve as an interesting introduction to the next chapter.

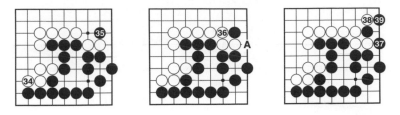

W34–W36 are the biggest moves for White. If White tried to play at *A*, Black would play at 36 and kill the three stones, so Black sets up a ko.

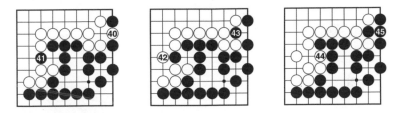

W40 takes, but Black has a ko threat at B41, which threatens a descent into White territory. W42 must block, but then Black can take back the ko. White takes with W44 and B45 fills the ko.

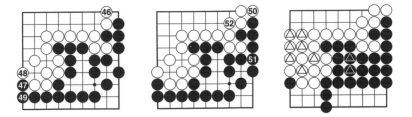

The last of the endgame moves follow. After the marked prisoners are put back on the board, Black has 16 points and White has 13 so, after komi, White wins by 3 $1/_2$ points.

As you can see, sacrifices can add a lot to your game and the bigger they are, the more interesting they become. Before trying to save a beleaguered group, always consider sacrifice. On the other hand, carefully consider the end results, since sacrifices are sometimes called *traps* or *swindles*.

CHAPTER THIRTEEN
A Big Ko

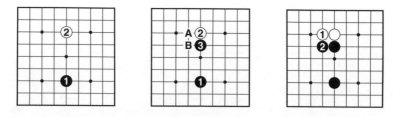

The opening stages of this fast TV professional game may look like a very quiet affair. Each side seems to be peacefully staking out territory along the top and bottom. However, the opposite is true because the center has been left open for high action.

B3 is an aggressive invasion that attaches to the White stone. There is a proverb that says, "Attaching to a stone will help it get stronger." This is a caution to beginners against playing too close to a stronger player's stone. On the other hand, looked at from the opposite point of view, with proper play, especially if sacrifices are involved, the invading forces will also gain strength. And the advantage of playing 9 x 9 Go is that close moves in the opening are often a necessity and you can learn faster that way.

White has two choices, *A* and *B*. *A* can be eliminated immediately. W1 in the diagram on the right is passive and over-desirous of territory, meaning that White would want to develop faster. No matter which way Black responded, White would lose too much of the board. Also, if Black chose to move along the top with White, the relationship between the emerging *wall* and the Black stone at the bottom would be ideal.

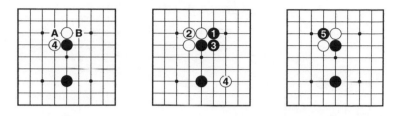

W4 is the only move. Next, with komi looming over the game, Black has only two choices, *A* or *B*. B1 would clearly be no good. W4 would set up a second group that Black would have trouble killing. It might be OK if every move could be read out, but this is fast Go! If White lived, White would win.

So Black *cross-cuts*. As you will see, there is no way to shake loose of this perhaps unwelcome embrace. When a cross-cut is used, it often creates a spectacular clash between local tactics and full-board strategies. The resulting balance or imbalance between immediate profit and long-term influence is one of the greatest things about Go. However, there are such a great number of responses that beginners often feel that cross-cutting or being cross-cut is like leaving one's fate to the gods. Thus, before we get to the main feature of this game—a really big ko—this section might require laying out the stones and/or several readings. However, once you have learned the essentials, your game will improve immensely because cross-cutting is one of the basic arts of Go.

Cross-Cuts

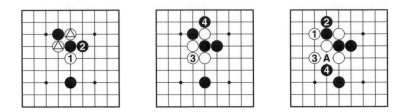

Now it is White's move and there are a number of bad choices available. If White tried an atari at the top of the formation, it would leave the two marked stones isolated. It would be very hard for White to keep both of them alive. The middle continuation leaves Black in control of most of the board.

While only amateurs would take the path shown in the right-hand diagram, it is instructive to see what they might find along it. In this variation, White would have induced all the upper Black stones to work together as a powerful group. Then the bottom Black stone could gather strength by *peeping*, or threatening to atari, at *A*, the defect in White's shape. Peeps are powerful tools worth remembering. They force the opposition into *bad shape* if they are filled, and if they are not, the aggressive atari can cause disaster.

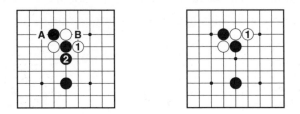

For White to atari the other way is worse! *A* and *B* are vulnerable points.

The best way of all, when caught in a cross-cut, is to make an *extension*. It is a powerful tool and generally makes things much easier. Think of it as putting a handle on a shovel, or using a lever to move a rock. As you will see later on, it is what White should have done in this game.

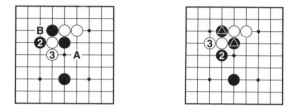

If Black ataris upward, White extends and a strong shape is formed. Black now has two problems. White has the potential to play at *A*, making a perfect mouth shape (see page 62). Black would have no escape. This is a method to remember! If Black runs out at *A*, then White attacks at *B*. If Black ataris to the side, one of the marked stones is dead or in deep trouble. It is evident that the sacrifices involved in these variations that start with ataris end up as dead losses so other ways should have been tried.

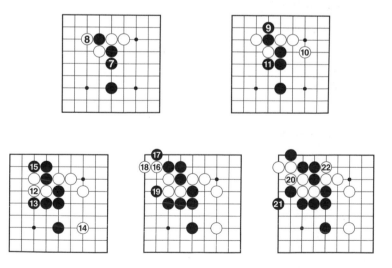

This one is OK for both sides, but this is a complicated game and the result is unclear. Still, this would be better for White than the way taken in the game.

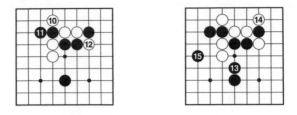

If Black runs along with White, the result is also unclear, but again White is better off than with the choice in the game.

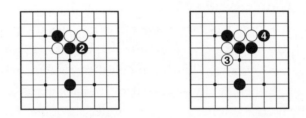

Here's another way. If White extends again, Black might fight back with the hane at B4; White might have to sweat a little but both groups would live. This result would also probably be better for White than in the game.

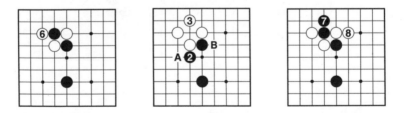

In the game, White ataris. It is perhaps not the best move, but it is absolute sente. Black cannot let that stone be taken because the resulting shape, called a *ponnuki* in Japanese, leaves moves like *A* or *B* available. With influence radiating all over the board, it would end the game. So a descent is made and White extends . . .

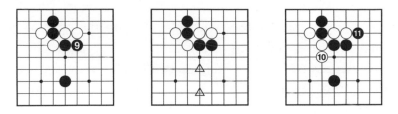

As Black moves along with White by playing B9, the distance between the small wall that is forming and the single stone below is ideal. It is easy to see that anything less or more would be too little or too much. The rule of thumb is that the number of intervening lines between a wall and its supporting stone should be one more than the length of the wall. Of course, the surrounding situation should also be taken into account.

Things start to change with the W10–B11 exchange. It is obvious that a sacrifice will take place for greater gains later on, but will it be the only one?

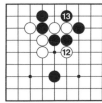
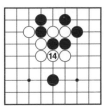
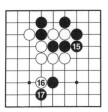

Next, W12 forces B13. W14 forces B15 because of the atari. This gives White sente to make a big move toward the bottom.

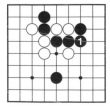
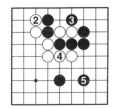
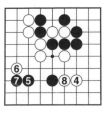

Why didn't Black just play B1? Wouldn't it create more power in the center? It is true Black would win if White played like this . . .

However, White would *set up shop* in the lower right. The Black stone is weak, and White would either live on the right or take enough territory on the left to win.

As mentioned before, setting up two living groups is usually a winning White strategy with komi involved. As on the big boards, the judgments of how aggressive to be are always set against territorial considerations.

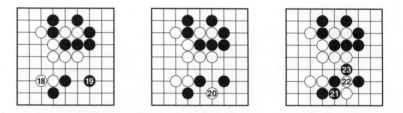

In this game, it is Black that has the opportunity to set up two groups by using standard techniques. White has two vulnerable corners on the left, and it looks like only one can be defended. However, these are professionals with deeper plans.

On the surface W20 might look unreasonable, and a beginner might wonder what White can hope to accomplish after B23.

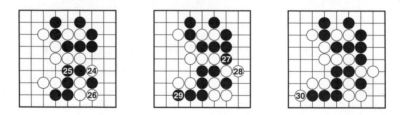

But events move quickly. After White creates a live group in the lower right, it is Black that now seems to be running out of room and just thrashing around blindly. Such are the changeable fortunes of Go warfare!

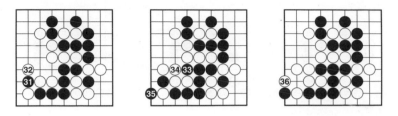

After B31–W34, Black makes a desperate move at B35 hoping that White will not notice a fatal flaw in this strategy to turn the game around by setting up a ko. Perhaps rushed by time, White unthinkingly takes. This is a lesson on why fighting spirit is so important—even professionals make mistakes!

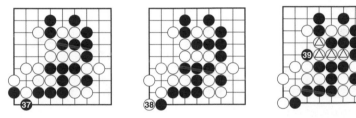

The ko is now unavoidable. White takes again but Black has the threat at B38 that puts the marked stones into atari.

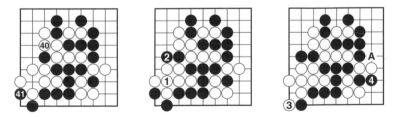

W40 eliminates the threat, but B41 takes back the ko. Usually the first thing to consider is filling the ko but here, as happened after B37, B2 would atari. If W3 takes, B4 makes the big threat to play at *A* and save the Black group.

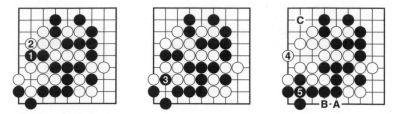

If White does nothing, Black is threatening to descend. White cannot fill because it would be atari. If W2, then Black takes with B3. It is atari! White would have to take and Black could fill with B5. This would mean Black has two eyes because if White plays *A* and Black plays *B*, White's corner is also vulnerable at *C*.

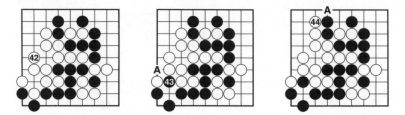

So White must take with W42, and this gives Black another opportunity. After Black takes, White must come up with a threat. But there is no threat big enough to prevent Black from taking at *A*, which would end the ko and save the group by making two eyes.

The best move White can muster is W44. This is big, however, because it prevents Black from invading the upper-right corner. Of course, it is nowhere near the size of the ko, but it is still enough to win the game.

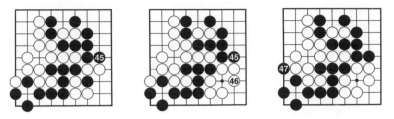

Before taking the ko, Black gets the big move in at B45. White must take with W46. So Black takes the final stone that ends the big ko.

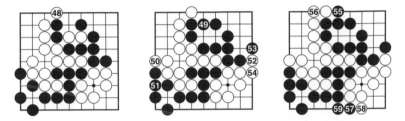

The small sente move of W48 is played. After all the excitement, only ordinary endgame moves are left.

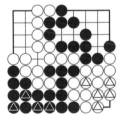
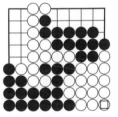

The marked prisoners are put down and the stones moved around to organize the empty intersections into units of five. The stone marked with a square is taken from the upper left in order not to miss counting the empty intersection in the lower right.

It is easy to see that Black has 11 points and White has 10, so, despite winning the ko, Black still lost by 5 $^1/_2$ points because of the komi.

After the heat of battle, players always find it useful to review their games. If it is possible, they will make game records to show stronger players, and to do this you can print your own recording sheets out from the AGA CD-ROM.

If a replay were done for this game, the reasons why some moves were dubious would have been revealed. The first is a mistake in *board management* that would be true for all sizes of boards. The second is another lesson in ko.

Hunting Down a Big Group

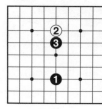
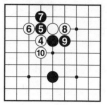
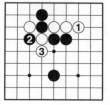

In small-board play, B3 makes sense. However, as you will see in chapter 14, invading so early in the game is generally not a good idea without making some preparations by putting down some supporting stones.

Next, instead of playing W10 toward the center, as in the second diagram, White should have responded by extending once more to the right.

B2 is the only response Black can make—any other play to try to save the right-side group would result in death. Even so, after W3, Black would be under heavy attack.

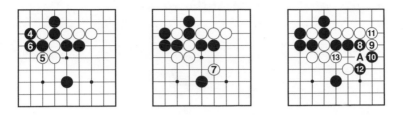

It would be relentless. If you were a tiger in ancient China, you would start to feel the nets entrapping you, hear the dogs howling and the shouts of men with spears not far behind! W13 threatens a snap-back at *A*.

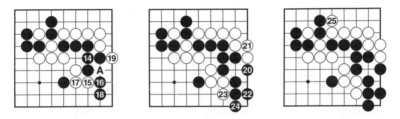

W19 would make a false eye at *A* so Black would live in gote, leaving White the sente move of W25 at the top. It would be time for Black to resign. White would be ahead by at least 10 points *on the board*, meaning White would be winning before komi is subtracted from Black's score.

When games get out of hand like this, it is always polite to resign and start another one. If you do this as a beginner, stronger players will enjoy playing with you much more. Generally, they will also tell you if they think you are making a mistake by resigning.

A Mistake in Ko

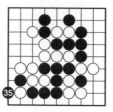

When Black tried to set up the ko with B35, White missed a killing move, but one that involved a different kind of ko. Can you see what it was?

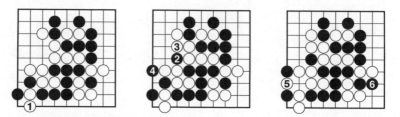

W1 is the correct move. Black is helpless. The only response is to try to make a ko with B4. White would take the ko and Black's only threat is B6, which endangers the corner.

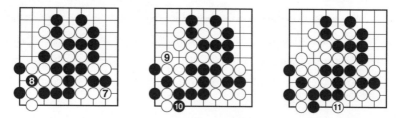

White would respond, enabling Black to take back the ko and put White into atari. W9 would take and it would be a hopeless situation for Black. W11 would be the coup de grâce. It would finish off Black, which would now have only one eye.

An Exercise

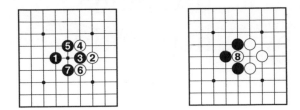

One playful and useful exercise to add a new dimension to your game is to play out this example from the first chapter on ko within the confines of a 9 x 9 board, with 6 $^1/_2$ points of komi. White can take so Black must find a ko threat. White can respond or fill the ko.

Try it without regard to being "correct" (since these are not the ideal moves to begin with), but to get acquainted with different kinds of ko threats, and what the effects of filling the ko at various moments would be for both players. Also, try to include the ideas of sacrifice from chapter 12 in your thinking. Then, investigate the idea of forming second groups as a convenient way of introducing the next chapter! You will see why 9 x 9 boards are so amenable to giving quick results in understanding and development!

CHAPTER FOURTEEN

Invading:
Why, When, and Where?

In the first game of this book, two large groups ended up vying for supremacy. This is a common event in games between beginning players, which made it a good teaching tool. However, in more advanced circles, where the players have a knowledge of invasion techniques, it is less common.

In multi-group games, fighting abilities, tactical prowess, and fighting spirit are usually more important than careful calculations about encircling the greatest amount of territory. To highlight the differences between these two approaches, two quick game reviews are offered that also illustrate how to open in the center. A lengthy explanation of a game that features a bold invasion follows.

Opening in the Center

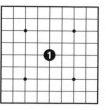

Opening on the central point is a powerful move in 9 x 9 Go. Unlike the last game, where the center was left open for maneuvers, B1 radiates power. Black will be able to attack *downward* in all directions.

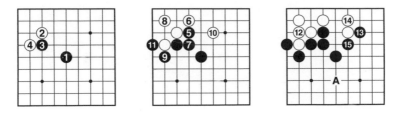

These are the opening moves of Game 4 on the AGA CD-ROM in the back of the book. Black was Go Seigen, perhaps the greatest player of all time.

Black's aggressiveness leaves White with no choice but to invade at *A* to establish a second group. You are invited to find out how this was done by playing out the rest of the game on the disk.

Opening on the center point of the big boards was explored by Go and others in the 1930s. These efforts were part of the *New Fuseki* ("New Opening Patterns") movement that swept through young, enthusiastic Japanese and imitative Chinese Go circles. The attacking style reminded them of (or perhaps was inspired by) the emerging techniques of aerial warfare. This is valid Go thinking and center plays are still made today because they embody the idea of establishing early influence to make later profit.

Playing at the center point on big boards also upsets thinking about joseki (standard, local corner openings that give balanced results for both sides). Complex coordination and lengthy experimentation are needed to play subsequent moves on the corners and sides, unlike 9 x 9 Go, where it is easier to understand the basic principles.

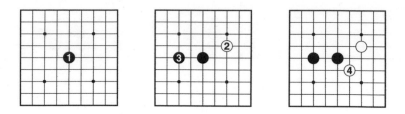

The center can also be used to squeeze the most profits out of the Go board. In this professional game, B3 suddenly draws back and assumes a seemingly defensive posture, much like the crouching tiger stance in martial arts. Sente no gote ("sente in gote") means making a gote move now in exchange for getting a bigger sente move later. It is the same kind of thinking involved in using an extension against a cross-cut, as demonstrated in the last chapter. In this game, the consequences are enormous because it is an invitation for a wholly territorial game. Any White stone played above or below it would be severely attacked.

Since there are no surprise moves, try to cover the diagrams with a piece of paper and guess the maximum profitable moves that follow.

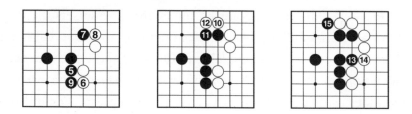

White accepts the invitation for a territorial game. By this time, professionals would have counted out every last point.

White plays W10 because it is sente and Black draws back, as if they were partners in a dance. Anything more aggressive on either side would end in disaster.

B13 is sente and threatens to cut through White. Next, the hane of B15 blocks off White's progress at the top.

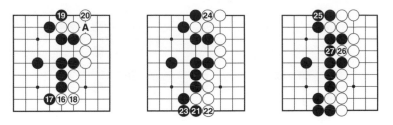

The remaining moves make up the endgame. As in the last game, W20 could be at *A*. White has 23 points and Black has 31. With a 6 $1/2$ point komi, White wins by a narrow 1 $1/2$ points.

Invasions

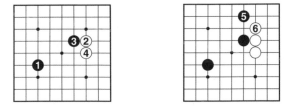

This fast TV professional game starts off in a similar fashion to the last game, with the board being divided up. However, this time, Black seems to want too much instead of not enough.

Another way of saying this is that Black is starting a *fast, loose* game, while White is playing a *slower, thick* one. These are contrasting styles of play. They are a matter of personality, preference, inclination, and intuition. The different styles of playing will become clearer if you leave yourself free to experiment with them.

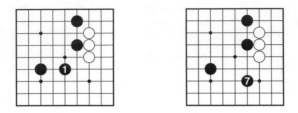

In this game, however, according to a more sober, post-game analysis, Black is playing a little too loose. White has a strong shape, so Black should probably try to make one, too, as B1 does in the first diagram. But Black plays B7—an overplay.

Confronted with such a defective, large structure, which seems to be laying claim to three quarters of the board, there is no question of peacefully reducing the size of Black's territory. White is invited or forced to invade.

As we saw in the first game in this book, the question of why, when, and where to invade is always interesting. Like the strategies and techniques that evolve from playing in the center first, it is critical that all the stones on the board work in unison for the attack to work. Then, depending on the outcome of the fighting, the question of retaining or losing sente becomes paramount. But where should White invade?

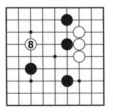

W8 seems to be the natural and perfect choice because it takes advantage of Black's open position. Closer to the top would not claim enough territory, and closer to the bottom would risk being undercut. In the first game of this chapter, there was no room for an invasion like this.

After the invasion, it is apparent how thin Black has become and how thick White is on the right. White's stone on the left can easily coordinate (perhaps "communicate" is a better word) with the wall on the right, where White does not have to worry about living.

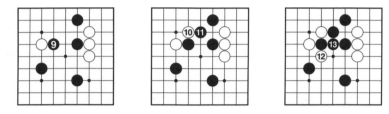

B9 is a *probing move* that leaves the decision of which direction to play up to White. White has the protection of the corner and sides, so W10 is played. The next set of moves follows naturally.

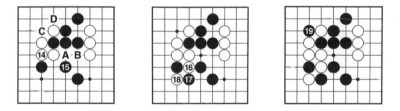

There is a delicate balance going on between defense and offense in this tight battle. Both sides must hold back their instincts for quick gain and patiently build up their positions, while keeping their alternatives as flexible as possible to adjust to later developments.

After White connects at W14, the single stone at the top seems to be left to its fate, but now, for safety's sake, Black must pay attention to the bottom. Also, White's connection at either *A* or *B* is threatened, so the big move for either player at *C* or *D* must wait. W16 is sente and, after W18, the White group is safe, but it is gote. With B19, Black gets the next big move in sente.

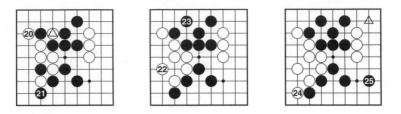

The battle for sente continues because the first move on the right side is going to be huge. Remember that one factor to consider about invasions is that, in order to stay alive or preserve territory, they often end in gote, as this one does.

Black gets a big move in at B25 (although the marked spot would have been slightly better). Nevertheless, the invasion strategy has so far been successful and White is ahead.

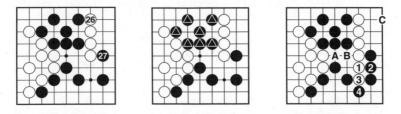

White and Black seem immune to fear as they attack each other with W26 and B27. This leaves four big questions swirling about the board. 1) Are the marked Black stones in danger? 2) How are their fates linked to whether White can or cannot connect at points *A* and *B*? 3) If there is no connection, will the isolated White stones die? 4) Even if White gets connected, can Black attack at *C* with a monkey jump. Would this destroy White's territory and win the game?

At this point in the game, nothing seems very certain, but that is the beauty of a complicated clash between contrasting styles of play. Fast development, even if slightly overdone as in this case, is not necessarily a bad strategy. By trusting in tactical prowess and fighting spirit Black induced an exciting, multi-group, fighting game. As the next chapter, and as the rest of the game will demonstrate, this is a good graduating exercise to the bigger boards and a good review of all that has gone before.

CHAPTER FIFTEEN

On to the Big Board: A Review of Go Basics

The last game was left in suspense with several groups that were *unsettled*. It has been a perfect example of the professional advice to "keep your options open until the last minute," and "don't settle your groups in gote," and "try to sweat out every advantage."

To see this clearly, however, you should lay out the stones to follow the action, then challenge your wits. (Please don't make the moves automatically but try to read things out.) In this way, your graduation to the bigger boards will become almost effortless.

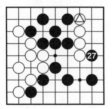 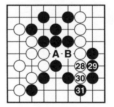

Black has just played the big move of B27 after White laid claim to the upper corner with the marked stone.

After the W28–B31 exchange, does it look like the White string of stones is in trouble? It does not seem possible to connect out because if White plays *A*, Black can block at *B* and vice-versa. Yet there is a way for White.

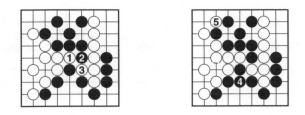

If White pushes at W1 and Black resists the attempt to link up, W3 puts Black into atari. After B4, Black has no answer to W5.

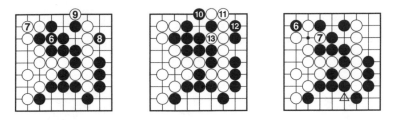

In this complicated *semiai*, after W5, Black cannot fill with B6 since White has more liberties than Black. If Black ataris, for example, White simply takes and has two liberties. If you don't understand this completely, try to lay out the stones. You will also see that Black cannot fight the ko, either. After W7, the only threat on the board belongs to White at the marked spot!

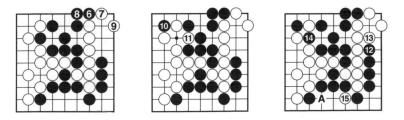

Nothing else works. Attacking with B6 on the right only results in a clever use of the dynamics of the corner to make an impenetrable two eyes. This is a handy thing to remember!

If Black persists by next playing ko with B14, White still has the ko threat at the bottom. Black would have no answer.

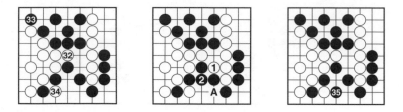

So, after White pushes, Black must play defensively to make two eyes. White doesn't connect immediately but has a bigger move at the bottom. Can you see it? The weaknesses of this kind of bad shape should be familiar now. White's follow-up at *A* would kill Black. Black has no choice but to play ko.

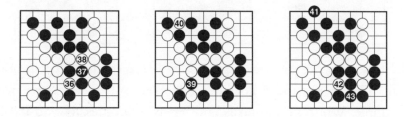

White takes and Black, with no big threats, defends. Now White can connect while putting the three Black stones into atari. Black can take back the ko, but White has a threat at the top. Black eliminates the threat, so White can take back the ko with W42 in gote. Black has no more threats, is in atari, and must submit to defending.

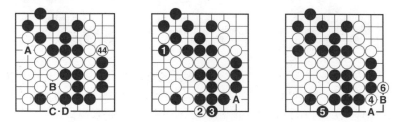

Instead of Black getting in a monkey jump, White can now make the significant territorial gote move on the right, assuring the victory. All that is left are endgame moves. But which is best for Black, *A*, *B*, *C*, or *D*? This will become an interesting exercise in corner dynamics.

If Black played on the left side, then W2 would create problems because the open position at *A* is always a vital point in corner formations. If Black persisted with B5 (instead of an atari of W4), W6 would be unstoppable! If Black *A*, then White's response at *B* could not be approached on either side! The stones and territory that White won would be added to the territory that Black lost. The total would far outweigh the few points that Black could gain.

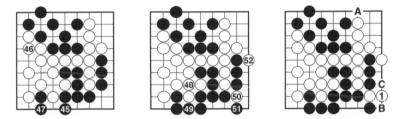

In the game, Black plays correctly—that is, conservatively—and White cannot cut off the stones at the bottom. To play W52 first would not be sente, so, as in the first game of this book, a sacrifice move of W50 keeps it going for White. If Black does not take the White stone in the corner, and plays at *A* instead, W1 descends and Black has no defense—*B* and *C* are self-atari.

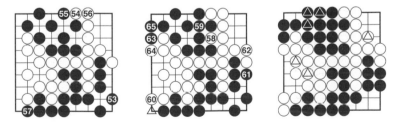

This gives White sente at the top and Black must fill. The rest of the endgame follows. The marked intersection is a dame.

Black has 10 points of territory but White has 12. Each has taken 3 prisoners, so it is a convincing 8 $^1/_2$ point win for White with komi. The game could have taken a different course several times (for example, at B15), but, because of the looseness of Black's initial position, it would not have made much difference. Still, the fighting was complex enough so each move had to be well thought out and precisely made.

Review this chapter once or twice, and if you have understood at least some of the techniques of this chapter, you are more than ready to tackle play on the larger boards!

Getting Started with Igowin

You may be coming to this section in one of several ways. If you have read through the book, you will be strong enough to skip to the last game, which serves as a review of the whole book. On the other hand, there are some good tips on handicap Go on all board sizes. There is also a short discussion about the worldwide rankings of Go players. This is how strangers playing on the Internet, in clubs, or in tournaments determine their handicaps for keeping things even and exciting.

Or after you bought the book, you might have been tempted to pull out the American Go Association CD-ROM and start playing immediately. You might also be somewhere in between, having read awhile and then gone on to Igowin and then back to here.

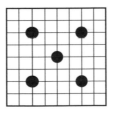

Igowin starts you out with five handicap stones placed on the *hoshi* or *star points*, marked by black dots on the board. (Think of the Go board as a map of the sky and the patterns of the stones as constellations as many in the East still do.)

Playing Igowin is like playing the old electronic game of Tetris—if you win, the handicap is reduced; if you lose, it is increased.

For those impatient ones who don't know already, a Go game ends when both players don't want to play anymore and "pass" their turns. The score of your first game with Igowin would have shown you that Go is a game of collecting empty spaces and the other player's stones. The one who ends up with the most "wins." But the question is, *why* did you win or lose?

After some games, you would figure out the basic premise of Go: that surrounded stones lose their "lives" and disappear off the board. If you count everything out, you will see that a stone that is taken off counts for 1 point and the empty intersection left behind also counts for 1 point. Lastly, you would have found that no situation can be repeated on the board. Igowin would tell you it was an illegal move and that another move has to be made first.

Next, after many, perhaps painful, games, you might figure out that surrounding empty space is more profitable than just surrounding and "killing" stones. After that, and many, many more games and lots of frustration, you might deduce that certain configurations of stones (called "groups") cannot be killed because, as Go players say, they have "two eyes." That is, a group of stones that has one space inside it can be "killed." Even though sometimes this act looks like a suicide move, Igowin will let you do it—the last empty inside intersection is vulnerable, but if there are two empty intersections (called eyes) the group is safe.

The next long step would be to painfully work out the idea that stones that are "attached" in certain ways to those safe groups are also "alive," and can greatly aid in the collecting of "territories" of empty intersections along with "captured" stones of the other player.

By then, you would have re-created the entire history of Go, something that could have taken centuries in history, and certainly wasted a lot of your time!

The easier way is to browse through the first six chapters of this book, or, if you really want to rush things, look at chapters 1,

2, and then 6, and also perhaps chapter 8. Either way, it won't take long and you will be smoothly sailing into Go playing.

Next, you will be ready to learn something about handicap Go strategies in this appendix, which will bring you up to playing even games with Igowin, which is a moderately strong player. With some more victories, you will be giving Igowin handicaps, a process that can be enjoyable for the rest of your Go playing career, even if you become quite strong.

All about Ranks

The word "wins" in the above section was deliberately put into quotes because, as all Go players know, winning is always a relative term.

In even games, Black always goes first, so points—called the *komi* in Japanese—are taken away for having that advantage. In the old, feudal days of Japan, there was no compensation given, so White was always played by the stronger player and "honor" was at stake—but how many points or how much honor has always been an arguable factor. In professional tournament Go since the 1920s, as players adjusted their styles, the amount of komi points that "democratically" evened up the games has mysteriously increased from $3\,^1/_2$ to $6\,^1/_2$ points. This has kept an overall 50 percent winning ratio for each side. In 9 x 9 Go, traditionally it has been $6\,^1/_2$ points.

In games between players who are not so evenly matched, one of the great glories of Go is the handicap system, which reduces all games to approximately even. This has translated into a world-wide ranking system.

Igowin starts you out with a rank of 25-kyu, the traditional beginning rank in Western Go. On the 19 x 19 board, this would mean, theoretically, that you would need twenty-five stones to play an even game with a 1-dan, a strength that is considered the benchmark of amateur achievement. The dan rankings go on up to between 6- and 8-dan, depending on the system used. The professional ranks begin at that level of skill and go from 1-dan up to 9-dan.

There haven't been any studies on the 9 x 9 board, but on the 19 x 19 board, in amateur play, a rank works out to be roughly equivalent to one handicap stone. So a 3-kyu would play even against a 4-kyu, who would have nothing subtracted for playing Black and going first. A 3-dan would give a 3-kyu six stones.

Generally, in the score of the first game two strangers play, say on the Internet, it seems to magically work out that 10 points difference in the score equals about one handicap stone. So if a player beats another player by 30 points, a good guess is that the next game should start with a three-stone handicap. Generally, after three wins in a row, or three out of four, the handicap should change one stone.

Professionals in Japan used to have a rating tournament, but now ranks are based on the number of winning games against other rated pros. Their rankings are different because the competition is so severe. A 9-P (a 9-dan pro) would give a 1-P only a stone or two and might even lose an even game once in a while.

It is interesting that worldwide amateur and professional rankings agree, once compensation is made for their relative strictness or laxness. For example, an American amateur 1-dan will not be as strong as a 1-dan on some of the Internet servers or in Europe, but these are all known factors. It is also interesting that, because there is no objective way to measure skill, the whole system has to be based on who beats whom, so, for the mathematically inclined, there are formulas used to prevent the automatic inflation of ranks over time.

Games with Igowin

It is important to point out that all computer Go programs have weaknesses that can be exploited, once humans figure them out. With full-size programs, in particular, this usually doesn't take too long, which is why all program rankings are suspect. They may be accurate for a few games, but then human minds are supple enough to create vagaries that will baffle them.

Much of the time, these tricks have little to do with good Go playing. If they were used against a human, they would be of little use. In keeping with the spirit that the Go board is one of the last places on Earth that humans can retain their dignity, Igowin is treated here as if it were human and reasonable Go playing were needed to win.

Also, please remember that this is advice for beginners, so the games presented here offer good, clear, general advice based on the general principles of good handicap Go playing, which are also valid on bigger boards. Long, complicated sequences that stronger players would use are not considered. In other words, thinking that beginners can comprehend is the key note for this section.

Another point is that Igowin, like any moderately strong player, likes to change things around, so don't expect exactly the same responses to the levels illustrated in this chapter. It is only the principles of good play that don't change.

25-Kyu

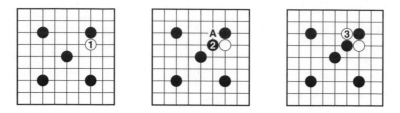

Three basic Go strategies are illustrated here. First, try to break up White's stones. Second, threaten to keep more territory than White. Third, if White responds by making two groups, attack only one. In other words, as in business, love, and war, try not to win everything.

After B2, Black threatens to play at *A* to confine White to one side of the board, so White tries to complicate things with W3.

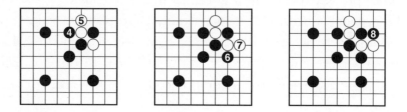

But Black is not afraid so White descends in self-defense. B4 repeats the maneuver, but White unwisely tries to save everything. Now Black can take either of the small White groups. If B8 is played . . .

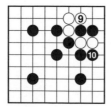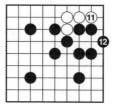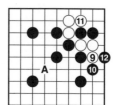

White has no defense.

Black can just ignore any White attempt to salvage what is left in the corner because the important point to note in these high-handicap games is that the rest of the board will continue to belong to Black. If Black is unsure about a second attack, a stone placed at or near *A* will always insure an easy victory.

18-Kyu

Just following that simple advice of giving White a small portion in return for getting a bigger one will bring you up to 18-kyu, when the help of the center stone and one corner stone is taken away. You are getting closer to playing real Go.

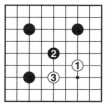 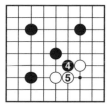 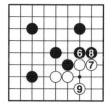

Following the same strategy of giving White something small in exchange for something big, Black takes control of the vital point at the center. This makes it effectively a four-stone game—usually a good policy. White starts to form a group along the bottom, but B4 pushes at the soft spot. This is good basic technique, too, because it pushes White down, limiting the amount of territory, while it strengthens Black above. Accomplishing two goals with one move is always a good idea! B6–W7–B8 completes the process. Black has good influence above while White has only a small amount of territory below. Next, Igowin makes a mistake. W9 is not needed. There is plenty of room to make eyes.

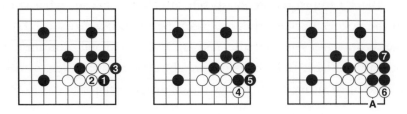

If Black attacked, White could easily get two eyes. *A* would make one and there is room for at least one more to the left.

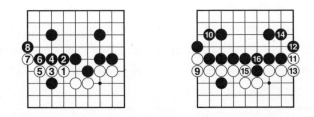

White could also just keep going, making territory, decreasing Black territory, and trapping the Black stone at the bottom. However, this strategy would still lose by about 10 points, and White would have no possibility of invading in the area around the marked square. Note the defensive moves of B10 and B14.

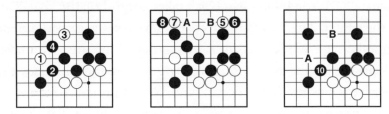

White could also try to invade instead of playing W9 in the game, but Black can easily foil these attempts by "dividing and conquering." If White tries to confuse the matter—to "muddy the waters" as the Taoist strategy advises—Black can atari at *A* or *B* and it would be all over for White.

In the game, taking advantage of White's mistake, Black can make the big move, so, in the end, White can only make a small territory at the bottom before resigning. There is no invasion, and that would have been White's only chance. However, as demonstrated, Black only has to cut off a stone at *A* or *B* and the game is over.

17-Kyu

At 17-kyu, still with a three-stone handicap but with a little more confidence in your fighting abilities, try an aggressive approach. Remember, you have all those stones to back you up and it is easy to resign and start over! Unlike humans, Igowin never gets tired and won't laugh at your mistakes.

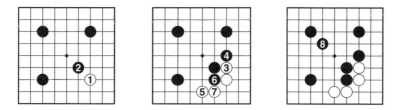

B4 is a hane at the head of two stones which is the recommended move to stop White's progress up the right side. B6 pushes down at White's weakness. B8 cements the victory. White can chip away at the edges, but there is no way that a group of stones can live inside the framework of the Black stones. You will find when you play handicap Go on bigger boards that frameworks like this are very useful for organizing large amounts of territory by making maximum use of the handicap stones.

16-Kyu

Notice how the victories are starting to pile up and how quickly you are moving down the kyu rankings. But remember that, as you advance, your progress will slow—each rank gets harder to advance through. That is the way of Go.

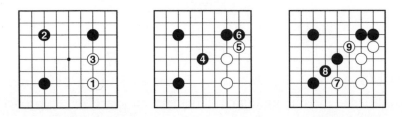

At 16-kyu, another stone will be taken off your handicap. Now, your armor is reduced to two and, although the principles are eternal, this new situation will require different strategies. Congratulations!

At two stones the kinds of questions that appear in Go on bigger boards with more open areas start to appear. The main idea is to first take control of the corner because you have the two edges to back you up when fighting. They will help you make territory.

Next, in 9 x 9 Go, playing B4 to take control of the center is vital. From the vantage of the center point, everything is "below" and vulnerable to attack!

There is a Go principle: "Keep White confined, and keep the Black stones connected." B8 is a natural expression of this concept. With W9, White also plays on a vital point, trying to isolate the small two-stone Black group in the upper right.

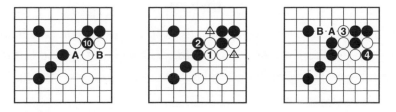

But Black is not afraid and B10 boldly pushes into White's thin position. A thin position is one that can be cut apart or penetrated. Now, White is weak at *A* and *B*.

If White connected at *A* with W1, after B2, White is weak at the marked spots.

For example, if White pushes with W3, Black can make one eye with B4 and has room in the corner to make another. White cannot push beyond *A* without being stopped by Black playing at *B*. Black has two large groups and White has only one small one. If White played at B4, Black would connect by playing at W3. Black's territory would be much larger than White's.

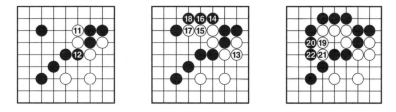

In the game, White decides to play W11, so Black naturally cuts with B12. White plays W13 to secure territory on the right side, but after B14, the game is essentially over. No matter where White's stones try to run, they can be captured. Again Black controls most of the board. Isn't Go easy?

15-Kyu

At 15-kyu you also have two stones. It is suggested you attach and try to complicate things. You may lose a few games at first, but the overall gain will soon be considerable.

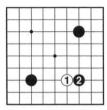 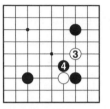 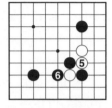

Igowin takes the bait. Igowin has learned from the 25-kyu game that it doesn't want to be holed up in the corner, so this time, W3 is tried. Boldly, Black cross-cuts anyway. W5 provokes B6, which threatens to capture.

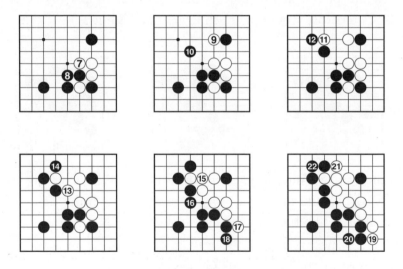

White must play W7 so Black's shape with B8 is very good for keeping White contained to the right side. It also works well with the lower-left handicap stone. By sacrificing the right side, there is little that White can do. Black simply contains White and common

Go sense dictates the rest of the moves for Black, who ends up with much more territory than White.

13-Kyu

At 13 kyu, you are close to playing even with Igowin and a radically different kind of thinking is called for since there will be more close maneuvering with less support. Thus, this game will serve as a review and also a preview of things to come when you start playing White. It asks the question, What happens when White wants to complicate things and make more than one group? For those who have read through the book, this question might remind them of chapter 14 on invasions. For those who haven't, it might seem a little complicated, but hopefully it will inspire them to do so.

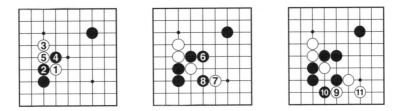

B6 splits White into two groups, one of which should die. Igowin tries W7—running would be foolish—but the strong shape puts the White stone under control. Next comes a series of shape moves. Go players would say each side is making shape—that is they're forming the stones into shapes that are easy to defend and can make two eyes. They are also flexible in that they can expand to make territory.

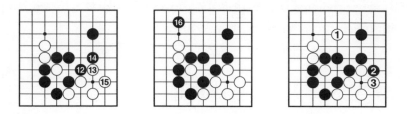

The shape moves continue, but the problem for Igowin is that
Black is getting stronger on the outside, and White is getting bot-
tled up in the corner. Black's strength sets up the killer move of
B16. White will not survive. If White tried to move on the top
first, Black would kill the bottom group. White could not fight the
ko—there are no threats big enough.

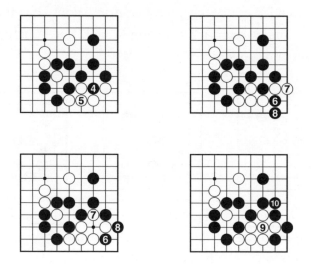

But if White protects . . . Black moves around White and still kills.
Either way White plays, two eyes cannot be made. Both these
plays feature clever moves called tesujis.

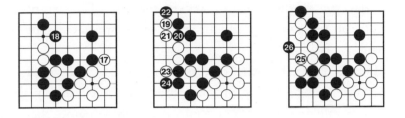

If White plays to say alive in the lower-right corner, the killing at the top proceeds. Black's shape is simply too good. And either way Black's play is useless. Note how B26 hits the vital point—this one is a point of symmetry, always a good place to aim at.

Getting Better at Go

Marked by a reduction in handicap stones, one's progress in Go is one of the mystifying features of taking up the game. But if cognitive psychologists and professional players haven't been able to figure out why some players get better more quickly than others, how can we amateurs understand it?

One factor to consider is style. Beginning players who are overly aggressive (or overly cautious) might win or lose against certain opponents of equal ranks who have the same (or opposite) styles. This is why player A might beat player B, who might beat player C, who, in turn, can beat player A, even though they are consistent against other players.

There is also the well-known "learning plateau effect"—many players advance quickly, then stagnate at a certain rank, then quickly advance again. Or one day you may feel strong and the next day you might lose to "weaker players." The ascent and descent of Go rankings can be even more spectacular playing Igowin.

This is often because players can become vulnerable for awhile after concentrating on one aspect of the game, but then, once this thinking is integrated into their whole game, they will zoom ahead. In other words, strategic concepts such as sacrificing, playing ko, thinking territorially, and invading, which were covered in the last chapters of this book, may take some time to be absorbed into your games. The best advice is to keep playing relatively fast games and experiment a lot! Be daring! Do not become obsessed with winning or your rank, or get too discouraged if you start to lose. Enjoy learning more about the game—it will enrich your experience of life!

Glossary

This list is by no means complete and is only intended to explain some of the Japanese and other foreign words commonly used in Western Go.

aji: (Ah-Gee) A condition in a position or group of stones that offers potential for play; aji may be good or bad.

atari: (A-Tar-Ee) A move that occupies the second-to-last liberty of an opponent's stone or group, thus threatening to capture it.

Baduk (or Paduk): (Ba Duke) The Korean word for Go.

dame: (Dah-May) Empty intersections left over at the end of the game that are of no consequence. Usually they are filled in by rotation.

dan: (Don) The highest section of rankings in Japanese and Western Go. Commonly used terms are: *Shodan*: a 1-dan; *Nidan*: a 2-dan; and *Sandan*: a 3-dan

fuseki: (Fu-Se-Kee) Somewhat formalized, full-board opening patterns.

gote: (Go-Tay) To play last in a local encounter; the opposite of sente. Gote loses the initiative.

gote no sente: (Go-Tay-No-Sen-Tay) Taking a step backward before striking in the martial arts; a gote move with a sente follow-up.

hane: (Han-Nay) A diagonal move played in contact with an enemy stone.

hoshi: (Ho-She) The nine star points on which handicap stones are placed.

Igo: (Ee-Go) The Japanese word for Go.

joseki: (Joe-Se-Kee) Semi-formalized corner sequences for opening big-board games.

ko: (Koh) A board position that requires a player to make a move elsewhere before recapturing after the opponent has just captured a stone, to avoid re-creating a former board position. One of the key strategic elements of the game. *Super-ko*: A simplification that resolves disputes over kos—no position is ever allowed to be repeated.

ko threat: A move that threatens something that a player makes before he or she is allowed to retake in a ko fight.

komi: (Koh-Me) The advantage for Black in going first is compensated by komi.

kyu: (Kee-You) The beginner rankings in Japanese and Western Go.

miai: (Me-I) Two points of equal value that do not directly affect each other. If one player takes one, the other player can take the other.

Nihon Ki-in: (Nee-Hon Keen) The chief Japanese Go Association, located in Tokyo.

ponnuki: (Pon-Nu-Key) An arrangement of four stones diagonally connected with a space in the middle. Said to be worth 30 points in the center.

seki: (Se-Kee) A position in which neither side can capture the other.

semiai: (Sem-Ee-Aye) A capturing race.

sente: (Sen-Tay) Sometimes called forcing moves; having the ability to choose where to play next. The opposite of gote. *Double sente*: Worth twice as much as a sente move because it is a sente move that also prevents a sente move of the opponent. *Reverse sente*: Approximately equal to a sente move because it prevents a sente move of the opponent.

Wei Ch'i (or *Wei Qi*, Mandarin, or *Wei Ki*, Cantonese): (Way-Chee) (Why-Kee) The Chinese word for Go. In the Chinese system of counting, no prisoners are taken and they are returned to their bowls. When no more plays are possible, all trapped stones are taken off the board and the remaining area and stones of one player are counted. If the total is more than $180 \frac{1}{2}$ (half of the 361 points of the Go board) plus or minus komi, then that player wins. Komi is $3 \frac{3}{4}$ points, half of the $7 \frac{1}{2}$ it might be if Japanese-style counting with prisoners and territories was used). There are other minor differences from Japanese rules. Stones inside a seki are counted and there is an advantage in playing last. Both rule sets prohibit suicide moves. Ko is also treated differently, but, as in Japan, the main idea is that no board position can repeat itself.

The "Ing Rules" are in a class by themselves. For much of his life, Ing Chang Yi, the great benefactor from Taiwan, tried to make a logical set of rules and insisted that they be used for some of the tournaments he sponsored. The komi is 8 points with Black winning ties, there are complicated ko and suicide rules, and extra time can be bought in exchange for points toward the end of a game.

Recommended Reading

Now that you've completed this book, you are more than ready to tackle play on the larger boards and the books that will teach you how. One is my own *Go! More Than a Game*, which is also game-oriented and, as a bonus, is the only book to include a full history of the game's incredible past, along with commentary on Go and modern mathematics, psychology, Western literature, and Taoism.

Kiseido Publications has the only series of books that can take one all the way up to respectable dan levels. Kiseido's site has the world's best Go-theme *ukiyoe* (Japanese "floating world" woodblocks) collection, which will soon be in book form. For the past twenty-five years, Kiseido (formally Ishi Press) has also published the magazine *Go World*, with lengthy commentaries and news of professional Go.

Janice Kim's Good Move Press has an excellent series of beginning books. Slate and Shell and Yutopian (which also publishes a small magazine, *Go Winds*) are the other major English-language Go publishers of excellent books. They are all on the Internet and all have worked closely for many years with the American Go Association. Their contact information can be found by contacting the AGA or going to their Web site at www.usgo.org, where an enormous number of other Web sites devoted to all aspects of the game of Go are also listed.

About the American Go Association

The American Go Association is the national organization of U.S. Go players, cooperating with similar national organizations around the world. As an organization we:

- Publish the *American Go E-Journal & Yearbook*. (You can sign up for the free weekly and bi-weekly journals at www.usgo.org.)
- Maintain a computerized rating system
- Sanction and promote AGA-rated tournaments
- Organize the annual U.S. Go Congress and Championships
- Distribute club and membership lists
- Schedule and organize tours of professional players
- Develop a strong national network of clubs
- Organize the Children's Go Camp
- Promote Go and enhance public awareness
- Strengthen the U.S. Go-playing community and its relations to other Go organizations in other parts of the world

There are AGA clubs in practically every major and many minor cities in the U.S. To find them, or to learn more about Go, contact:
American Go Association
PO Box 397
Old Chelsea Station
New York, NY 10113-0397
Tel: 917-817-7080
www.usgo.org

9 x 9 Board

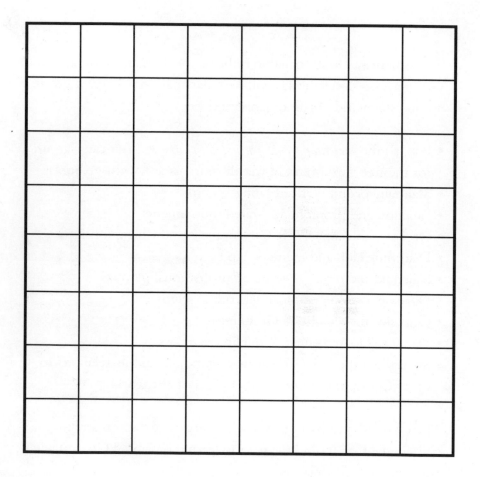